MUST BRETHREN CHURCHES DIE?

This book is a compilation of four addresses given by Dr. Kevin G. Dyer at conferences for church leaders.

Dr. Dyer, founder and former president of International teams, a short-term missions agency, now serves as chairman of its Executive Council. He is a former missionary, and in addition to his leadership in missions, is a catalyst for church growth and renewal.

Must Brethren Churches Die?

by Kevin G. Dyer

introduction by
JOHN ALLAN

PARTNERSHIP

AUSTRALIA:
Bookhouse Australia Ltd.,
P.O. Box 115, Flemington Markets, NSW 2129

British Library Cataloguing in Publication Data

Dyer, Kevin G.
    Must Brethren churches die?
    I. Title
    262.72

ISBN 0–900128–08–9

Typeset in Great Britain by Photoprint, 9–11 Alexandra Lane,
Torquay, Devon and printed for Partnership, 3 Mount Radford Crescent,
Exeter, Devon by Wheatons BPCC, Exeter

Contents

Introduction

'A New Shape, Though Unformed'

John Allan

BOOKS don't always achieve very much. In the present climate in Britain, where the market is flooded every month by far too many titles anyway, that is especially obvious. It is sad to see how easily a good Christian book can be overlooked—its message drowned out by the clamour of other, glossier, more enthusiastically promoted productions.

But every so often a book comes along which really makes a difference. A book which quietly starts a revolution, because it chimes in uncannily well with what people need to hear. It echoes the dilemmas and questions and tentative conclusions which are already forming in their minds, and moves on beyond them to suggest some startlingly simple solutions.

I very much hope that this book will have such a career. And especially among the Brethren fellowships whom Kevin Dyer knows best; but more broadly among independent evangelical churches which are stuck in a rut, or in danger of going that way. Kevin Dyer says things which need to be heard, clearly and penetratingly, by leaders in evangelical churches all over the British Isles.

This is not some new form of the charismatic package. A reader can believe what he likes about things charismatic, and still profit from Dyer's observations. The four sections of this book simply reflect good practical biblical sense about churches, the way in which they need to be led and managed, and the terrible possibility of operating on expectations of defeat and a 'survival' philosophy.

For most of this century, British evangelicals have had small expectations, even if their rhetoric hasn't always suggested it.

We have been in the background of major church debates, while liberals and Catholics have dominated in intellectual and political controversy. We have seen steadily declining numbers from the First World War onwards; throughout the twentieth century, most British pastors have experienced only a shrinking congregation as they have grown older.

We have been abandoned in greater and greater numbers by the young. We have failed almost totally to win the inner cities for Christ, the ethnic minorities, the rural villages. Even those denominations which began with a 'working class' feel—such as the early Pentecostal groups, or the Brethren in the North—have gradually become more and more socially successful. As the number of cars outside mission halls has increased, and chartered accountants and teachers have replaced miners and fishermen inside, evangelical groups have become more and more middle class. There is a broad swathe of this country's population which is more remote from evangelical Christianity than ever before.

Suddenly in the sixties, in the midst of this scene of defeat, there erupted the charismatic movement. And that has changed everything. It has catapulted evangelicals back into the limelight, brought them together in new and startling liaisons, broken down historic divisions, and created a boldness in evangelism which has planted churches and established missions all over the world.

Charismatics and others

For those who have been touched by the charismatic movement, one of the greatest benefits it has brought has been the sense that God is a God of movement and change, whose purposes for us are exciting and who demands flexibility from a people whom he loves to surprise. Churches influenced by charismatic thinking have tended to experience a loosening-up in their structures, a new hunger for closeness and open sharing between individual Christians, the emergence of new gifts of leadership with an emphasis upon big, bold, audacious visions. One church which has enjoyed massive growth adopted as its motto, 'Constant change is here to stay'.

But what about those evangelicals who—for good theological reasons, in many cases—have found the charismatic 'package' unacceptable to them? And what about those who have adopted the style and image of the charismatic movement (singing the songs, listening to the tapes, copying the structures) without any real deep and lasting change seeming to arrive? All too often, churches in these positions have found themselves increasingly stranded. It is as if they are becalmed on their own traditional island while the tide of church history surges irresistibly by. Is there any hope for them? Or must they simply die out?

It is to churches with these problems that Kevin Dyer addresses himself. Churches which are traditional not for the sake of it, out of stubbornness and bigotry, but where there is a real desire to do God's will and see his name glorified; yet where, somehow, it just isn't working. Churches where there are memories of past glories, days when God's Spirit seemed to be picking up his people and thrusting them forward from one spiritual adventure into another—but where the memories are only memories. Churches, in short, like the typical Brethren assembly.

The Brethren: a terminal case?

No group of evangelical churches has experienced a more ruinous decline over the last few years than the Brethren. The figures show that today the Brethren are a rapidly ageing group with a limited investment in the future (only about half of their churches can boast a youth group), and with a recent sad history of church closures, one after another, as older people have died off and younger families have gravitated towards the more lively atmosphere of Anglican or Restorationist circles. The number of ex-Brethren in leading positions throughout the evangelical world is impressive, and it proves two things: first, that the Brethren *have been* a terrific training ground for leaders and scholars; but second, that they won't be much longer, since most of their brightest and best are leaving them and going elsewhere. I speak as someone who was once the only Brethren member of the (nine-strong) leadership team of British Youth for Christ. No less than seven of the others had been Brethren . . . once.

To some people it might appear that the onward movement of history has simply left the Brethren behind, and that the realistic thing to do might be to shut up shop, join up with a cause which *is* going somewhere, and give up trying to breathe life into an incorrigibly dead donkey. For some small, struggling 'Gospel Halls', indeed, that might well be the best solution; it is not faithfulness to God, but a willingness to subject the gospel to mockery and derision, that keeps open the door of a tiny 'tin tabernacle' with only two or three members when across the road there is a thriving evangelical church which would love to absorb the stubborn few into its fellowship.

But there are other churches where shoots of new life have begun to appear. In a recent article in the magazine *Aware*, Dr. Harold Rowdon has christened these churches 'reborn' Brethren assemblies:

> Well over a hundred is my guess, with perhaps as many again beginning to come to birth. If this estimate is anything like correct it constitutes something approaching 20% of the total number of Open Brethren churches in the U.K.

In 'reborn' Brethren churches, the mould of the past has been broken. Instead of meekly conforming to the traditions of former days, and allowing them to shape every aspect of the life of the congregation and its members, leaders of 'reborn' churches question everything that is not biblically essential. They are learning increasingly to make the distinction that Kevin Dyer makes in this book (pp. 28–30) between 'fundamentals' (which are completely non-negotiable), 'distinctives' (which typify the Brethren tradition, but shouldn't be used as pretexts for an unscriptural shunning of other kinds of believers), and 'secondary issues' (on which believers in the same fellowship can differ, without forfeiting unity and mutual trust).

So evangelism is an inescapable necessity; but the 6:30 p.m. 'Gospel service' is not. And 'one man ministry' is to be avoided, since we hold firmly to the priesthood of all believers; but that need not prevent us recognizing that some have the gift of teaching, and others don't, or even employing one suitably gifted person to provide the core of a church's teaching ministry.

Non-Brethren Brethren

The 'reborn' churches have been forced to undertake this total review of practices and beliefs by the very fact that their churches tend to be made up more and more of Christians who come from *non*-Brethren traditions! In my own church, members may have any kind of background—we have former Anglicans, Baptists, Pentecostals, Restorationists, Presbyterians, Methodists, who have come to us not because of our denominational slant, but simply because we are a large and lively fellowship in which they felt very much at home. And this is happening throughout Britain increasingly today: Christians are choosing their church not on the basis of rigid traditional loyalties, but by asking, 'Is this a church where I can feel at home? Will I be spiritually fed? Can I make a contribution and fulfil my potential for God here?'

It is an exciting situation to be in, for it recalls irresistibly the first days of the Brethren—when a loose amalgam of Christians from widely differing church backgrounds came together to hammer out something new: a return to 'primitive Christianity', the simplicity of the absolute basics. Their only common ground for discussion and argument was the Word of God. But the history of the Brethren movement shows how early the new movement became bogged down in dogmatism and dispute. Perhaps, a hundred and fifty years on, God is giving us another chance.

The Brethren have an outstanding place in the history of parachurch movements. It is remarkable how consistently they have produced men and women of vision who have been able to build international missions, found evangelistic agencies, create unpredented projects and enterprises and movements. Partly this has been because the atmosphere of the local church has often been so restrictive—and the opportunities for creative thinking by members so limited—that the entrepreneurs have been thrust out into the interdenominational world, to work out their plans untrammelled.

In some ways, Kevin Dyer is a typical example. The founder and former president of International Teams, he has succeeded in building a ministry which has thrust literally thousands of ordinary Christians out into missionary service in a quite unparalleled way. And looking at the Brethren churches he knows and loves, he has felt deep frustration and dissatisfaction at their record of decline and low expectations. But unlike many others, he hasn't yet written off the small evangelical church. He believes that revival and rebirth are possibilities; he has seen them happen. And he longs to see them happen more often.

Two views on unity

What are the essential elements in a church's 'rebirth'? Dyer analyzes four. The first is *unity*, which has never been an easy subject for Brethren thinking to sort out. From the earliest days of the movement we have inherited two competing strands of teaching: first the warm, accepting, inclusive vision of unity which characterized men like George Muller, R.C. Chapman, and Anthony Norris Groves, who said:

> I feel every saint to be a holy person, because Christ dwells in him, and manifests Himself where he worships; and though his faults be as many as the hairs of his head, my duty still is, with my Lord, to join him as a member of the mystical body, and to hold communion and fellowship with him in any work of the Lord in which he may be engaged.

But, second, there was also the strand of teaching which developed from the complex thinking of J.N. Darby, and bore later fruit in Exclusivism, the 'Needed Truth' movement and other Brethren offshoots: the stress upon 'the truth of separation', the horror of drifting into 'sectarianism' by contact with Christians in other denominations, and so encouraging 'apostasy'. It is this second strand which has sadly proved more dominant in Brethren affairs this century.

Kevin Dyer argues that we need to lay the ghost of Brethren separatism. The only kind of church which God will bless is the one which recognizes the unity of all believers, and refuses to disown any of the ways in which God goes to work, however much they disappoint our preferences. Sometimes this may mean risky alliances; but the risk is worth taking, as Anthony Norris Groves saw clearly right at the start of the movement:

Yet as to our liberty in Christ to worship with any congregation under heaven where He manifests Himself to bless and to save, can there be in any Christian mind a doubt? . . . To the question, Are we not countenancing error by this plan? our answer is, that if we must appear to countenance error, or discountenance brotherly love, and the visible union of the Church of God, we prefer the former, hoping that our lives and our tongues may be allowed by the Lord so intelligibly to speak that at last our righteousness shall be allowed to appear . . .

When an evangelical church shuns the pursuit of unity, distortions and defects start to appear in its life. First, as became obvious very early among Darby's group of followers, there is a blurring of the distinction between 'fundamentals', 'distinctives' and 'secondary issues'. Minor practices become just as binding, just as obligatory, as major beliefs. In fact, they almost become more important; more battles have probably been fought in Brethren circles over trivial issues than over key points of doctrine.

Second, the community of the church ceases to be the sort of group that people can easily attach themselves to; and evangelism wanes. If it is through our love that outsiders will know that we are Christians (John 13:35), the harder it becomes to spot, the less likely they are to see Christ in us. Unbelieving adults typically come to faith by entering the atmosphere of a loving Christian community, seeing something there that cannot be explained in purely human terms, and gradually becoming convinced of the reality of Jesus Christ because of the reality of his life in his people. But a separatist church cannot afford to let other people come too close to the charmed circle of its fellowship; and so people may respect the Christians for their beliefs, admire their morally principled lives, and value them as neighbours, but never for a moment dream of joining their community.

Another distortion that disunity has engendered among Brethren churches (and Strict Baptist ones too, according to some of their leaders) is the myth of the *independence of the local church*. Kevin Dyer warns, 'Autonomy is not the same as independence . . . We are in serious danger today of becoming cultic about independence.' There are some things that local churches can do best on their own. There are other things that they do better jointly; and to insist fanatically on local church independence to the point where we are unable to work together, is to weaken the impact we can have upon the world for God.

Yet, sadly, the impression many other Christians have of the Brethren is that we are impossible to work with, suspicious of everyone else, clannish and superior in our attitudes. And often we miss out on resources which are available to our churches in the wider Christian world—training, information, consultation, representation—simply because we are scared of working together. We are frightened that if we do, we will lose our identity and become just a part of some organization. Yet, as Harold Rowdon has pointed out in his *Who Are The Brethren— And Does It Matter?*, even in the earliest days of the church there is evidence of inter-church cooperation and association.

I am a youth worker, and as I look at the good work being done in Anglican circles by Church Youth Fellowships Association, in the URC by the Fellowship of United Reformed Youth, and in the Assemblies of God by their National Youth Council, I feel frustrated that no comparable service agency exists to pick up Brethren youth work by the scruff of the neck and introduce it to excellence in the same way. Or tracing the impact of ginger groups such as GEAR in the United Reformed Church, Mainstream among Baptist Churches, and the Anglican Evangelical Fellowship in the Established Church, it is tantalising to imagine what a similar groundswell movement could do for the Brethren.

To wish for these things is not to slip into becoming 'denominational'. There's a difference between the kind of New Testament association of churches for which Harold Rowdon pleads, and the rigid central control which Brethren dread. Already Brethren have a long history of distinguished co-operative efforts (Counties Evangelistic Work, area conferences, regional youth camps); and in some parts of the country— Suffolk is a distinguished example—elders of churches have started to meet together for their mutual benefit. Pursuing unity isn't an option; for a small independent church, it's a vital factor in maintaining health.

Leaders and elders

After unity, Dyer goes on to talk about *leadership*. This is one topic on which views in the evangelical church have changed dramatically in the last few years. Anglican and Baptist churches have begun to appoint elders, and adopt a style which allows much more lay participation than ever before; Brethren have begun to appoint full-time workers and to recognize the work of deacons as well as elders. Among Restorationists, various forms of leadership have emerged, with categories such as 'apostle' becoming a seriously-worked-out reality. The leadership potential of women has been hotly debated, and accorded wildly varying degrees of recognition in different places. Young people have increasingly emerged into leadership more than ever before.

Perhaps because of the charismatic loosening-up, perhaps because of the economic recession, it has become increasingly common for Christian leaders to be 'full-time workers' for a number of years, then to go back into secular employement—or even to shuttle from one role to the other. The upshot is that the aura of awe which in some circles surrounded full-timers (who had been specially called for life by God to this work) has dimmed a little. Full-time work—especially in an age of short-term service opportunities—may be a high and holy calling, but it isn't necessarily so out of the ordinary that it elevates the person concerned into a specially important position of influence.

This is healthy for groups like the Brethren, who have often been unduly controlled through the years by peripatetic teachers and evangelists who exercised a great deal of unrecognized authority over local congregations, not *always* for the good. It was dangerously possible for the full-time men of God to be regarded as an elite caste with special resources of wisdom and authority. (I remember when I was a boy listening to one old lady's verdict on my father, after he had preached in her church: 'He's a *conference speaker*,' she said, reverently, 'he's far too good to take our meeting.')

The challenge today is to recognize that full-timers and part-timers equally have a contribution to make, within the corporate leadership team of a church; and to structure things so that neither type of leader prevails over the other. (There have been situations where the 'staff meeting' of full-timers has taken all the important decisions, rendering the other elders meaningless; and situations where the elders have regarded their full-time brethren as hired employees, and therefore of inferior status in decision making, whether they were doing the work of an elder or not.)

But Kevin Dyer throws out another challenge. He calls us to recognize a distinction between 'leaders' and 'elders'. Not all elders have the gift of visionary planning and creative discernment. Not all leaders have the pastoral, teaching abilities of a good elder.

Is this a biblical distinction? Anyone who has sat through a slow-moving, indecisive elders' meeting will be immediately interested! And, equally, anyone who has experienced the headlong, impatient rush of new developments when impetuous leaders are unrestrained by pastoral considerations, will appreciate that this distinction isn't imaginary. Leading is one thing. Shepherding the flock is another.

Years ago, Ted Engstrom made a similar distinction in his renowned book *The Making of a Christian Leader*. He was talking about para-church organizations, but the same principle applies to local churches:

> Because leadership is an attitude as well as an action it must be distinguished from management. While there are certain functional similarities in both leadership and management, leadership has distinctive characteristics. It is unfortunate that so often little attention is given to these distinctives in developing organizational philosophy . . .

Peter Wagner's book *Your Church Can Grow* has had an enormous influence upon churches around the world. It sums up 'seven vital signs' of growing churches, and the first of the seven is 'a pastor who is a possibility thinker'. One of Wagner's chapters is headed 'Pastor, don't be afraid of power!' and in it he tells the stories of pastors who have seized decision-making power from slow-moving committees and consistories, and have experienced tremendous church growth as a result. One of his examples was Donald Hamman of Chicago:

In effect, Donald Hamman was saying to his congregation that Medinah Baptist had a great opportunity for growth ahead, but that if the church wanted to grow it had to streamline its decision-making process. It had to get rid of the bulky and cumbersome committee structure. It had to implement the principle underlying this whole chapter: *the pastor has the power in a growing church.*

Many brethren, and other independents, would recoil instinctively from this cheerful ecclesiastical totalitarianism (although it isn't all that far from the autocracy practised in early Brethren history by Newton at Plymouth, for example). Do we not believe in corporate leadership? Yet Wagner's observation contains an important truth: that dynamic leadership can never come from a broadly-based committee whose gifts are primarily pastoral. A small group of leaders (if not one omnipotent pastor) can take a church much further much faster than the traditional style of management we have evolved.

(And we should remember that the 'traditional style' of Brethren leadership is much less uniform than we sometimes imagine. There have been many different styles—ranging from full congregational control by a 'brothers' meeting' to complete domination by one or two leading elders. As many as nine different normative Brethren patterns of leadership have been distinguished!)

So what is Dyer's chapter saying to us? Readers will disagree about how firmly the leadership/eldership distinction is rooted in Scripture—is it a neglected New Testament principle, or just a useful practical observation? And in different situations it may have to be worked out differently; a lot depends upon the size of the congregation which we are trying to manage. But the challenge of this chapter must not be ducked. Unless we recognize who our leaders are, and set them free to lead, our church life will die the death of a thousand qualifications.

Leaders change things

'Leadership provides direction,' says Olan Hendrix; 'management is about control.' Leadership, in other words, thrusts forward into the future; management concerns itself more with the present state of affairs. If our churches liberate leaders a little more, *change* becomes inevitable. Leadership is not leadership unless it's leading you somewhere you haven't got to already.

We need change, says Kevin Dyer. 'In most churches we are going through the motions. We are playing church. There is little evidence that God the Holy Spirit is doing much among us.'

Why do we shy away from change? Partly it is that in the course of the twentieth century our tradition has become obsessed with doing things properly—'See that thou do all things according to the pattern shown thee in the Mount' has become a much-misapplied text! We have developed a stifling conformity in our ways of doing things, which has straitjacketed us (until comparatively recently) into an unmistakeable Brethren style from which it has been unthinkable to stray. We are not the only ones; other denominations naturally tend to evolve a 'house style' too; but because we have often convinced ourselves that our ways of church government and ordering are New Testament-ordained, we have been more reluctant to countenance changes than anyone else.

We need to have the humility to accept that not everything we have called 'church truth' is straight from the New Testament. The basic principles can be applied in different ways to fit different cultures and different centuries. And the constant challenge to us is to remould our understanding again and again, as situations change, while still remaining faithful to the basic convictions that underly our practices.

But another reason for our resistance to change is much simpler and more human. All change—even good change—causes stress. Too much change too quickly threatens us. And so we naturally prefer to stick with the imperfect reality we know already, than risk launching ourselves out into an uncertain future which might be far better.

But Christians are called to have faith. We are the spiritual descendants of Abraham, who left all he knew in Ur to seek for a city which had foundations, whose builder and maker was God. The church with a positive attitude to change is the church which God can work with. It is a church which finds its security only in him and his Word—not in well-loved patterns of worship, traditional phrases, accustomed times of services, 'safe' numbers on a Sunday.

Kevin Dyer talks about the attitude we need to cultivate in order to handle change without fear. He also discusses the best way to bring change about—in a brief four-point section that should be read again and again by elders all over the country. For change can be destructive as well as life-bringing; and the correct changes, applied in an incorrect way, can spell disaster.

Unless we recognize three basic facts about change, we're doomed before we start. First, change is inevitable. It will happen whether we want it or not; because none of us can stand still. The only choice is whether it is good change or bad change. Those Brethren who try still to recreate the assembly conditions of fifty years ago—with hats, dispensationalism, annual conferences and unaccompanied singing—are increasingly finding themselves incapable of doing it. History is passing them by, and if the great men of the past came back (the J.B. Watsons, the W.E. Vines) they would not recognize the pitiful survival as anything remotely resembling the churches they used to know.

Second, change is imperfect. No one change will bring about the ideal situation of which we dream. And so change is a matter of accommodation and perpetual negotiation; moving no faster than people's fears and questions will allow, keeping the church united at the same time as stretching its faith and courage to the limit. Leaders have a tendency to glimpse the far horizon and then surge forward to try to reach it instantly. That's why they need elders; otherwise they may storm ahead to the promised land, and find they arrive there on their own. The church has abandoned them somewhere on the journey.

Third, change is perpetual. Some small churches have made the mistake of assuming that one big upheaval, one wholesale reform, is needed in their church life. After that, it will be plain sailing. But one of the few permanent features in church life is impermanence! We never reach the perfect state. There is always more to be done.

But unless this principle is firmly grasped by everybody, some who have reluctantly bowed to an initial set of changes will sooner or later become aggrieved. 'We gave in and let you make all these changes last year,' they will say. 'We thought that would satisfy you. But now you want *more* changes too! Do you want to change everything? Where will it end? We don't recognize this as our church any longer.'

To which, of course, the only answer is: quite right, it never was your church; it belongs to the one who stands in the midst of the seven golden lampstands. And he alone knows 'where it will end', for he alone is the first and the last, the one who is alive for evermore.

And this leads Kevin Dyer naturally into his final point. *Vision* is the one quality which will make unity, leadership and change a life-giving reality. Unless we 'get off our seats and dream and plan creatively', none of the rest of this argument will make any practical sense at all. Dyer quotes the devastating comment of Helen Keller: 'The greatest tragedy to befall a person is to have sight but lack vision.' And then he adds, 'That's true of churches too.'

It is not difficult to see the problems. Leaders of small evangelical churches typically spend hours discussing, analyzing and pin-pointing the precise nature of their malaise. Brethren especially have an irresistible fascination with navel-gazing: the number of letters, articles and comments submitted to *Aware* magazine on the ills of the Brethren movement far outweighs those on any other topic. But seeing the problem does not imply having the courage to do anything about it.

What do you see when you dream?

I see a vision of renewed, independent, small centres of life and joy all over the country, spreading ever outward in a colourful mosaic of creativity and vitality, laughing at the hidebound structures of lumbering denominations and rejoicing in the freedom of local diversity. I see congregations reflecting the local culture of their area—an Asian flavour in Handsworth and Southall, a West Indian style in Brixton and Dudley—yet united in conviction and mutual respect, coming together to support joint projects expressing Christian love and caring evangelism in unfashionable sectors of British society. I see a revival of Brethren scholarship, and a hunger for knowledge of

God's Word that mutually grips postmen and post-graduates, lorry-drivers and lecturers as they all meet together around bread and wine.

I see a tidal wave of young people filling our churches, enlivening and upsetting them constantly, finding in them a style and a freedom which is relevant, affirming, twenty-first-century, real. I see women released into ministries which fulfil and satisfy them and their families, playing their full part in the body of Christ for the first time in centuries. I see a massive Brethren missionary initiative as the renewal in this country spills over into a concern for less fortunate cultures, and a selfless volunteering of lives and resources by a whole new generation of F.S. Arnots and F.W. Baedekers. I see, too, a networking of all these shoots of new life in a careful, sensitive way, which enables them to support energetically and contribute sensitively to the total work of God in this country, resisting any temptation to isolationism and pride, recognizing and affirming all God's people wherever they are.

But can it ever happen?

It must have seemed an equally crazy vision when a few young men in the nineteenth century left the shelter of the established denominations they had always known to start meeting together in a simpler, more biblical way. What hope did they have of initiating a worldwide renewal? How could they even begin to rewrite two thousand years of church history? What were they in the face of the overwhelming odds against them?

Yet they believed they had a vision from God, and must be faithful to it. And so before long, as Darby wrote excitedly in 1833, 'things are assuming a new shape, though unformed, and there will be an entirely new state of things in a year or two'.

Kevin Dyer wants to ask: is there any reason why, just one hundred and fifty years later, we should not be able to use those words again?

Chapter 1

Father, Make Us One

I come from the state of Tasmania in Australia. In a small town not far from where I lived there is a beautiful stone church. The hand-cut stone is magnificent and the architecture is outstanding. As the church towers skyward, everyone can see this beautiful landmark.

The church was built back in the 1880s when many people in the small town got together and worked on the church. Some cut stone, others laid them, while still others worked on the stained glass windows. It was a united effort . . . amazing in the fact that many people from different backgrounds helped build this church.

When they got to the top of the walls and were ready to put the roof on, an argument broke out. People took sides. The work stopped and division swept through the congregation.

The roof was never put on, and for 90 years that church building stood incomplete without a roof. Four generations were born and died. Children wondered why the church was never finished. Young people could not believe that it stood incomplete. About 15 years ago they finally got together and finished the church.

But for 90 years it stood as a terrible testimony to division and disunity.

That is a local church, but the Church universal is also greatly divided. There are more than 24 varieties of Baptists in the United States of America. There are 15 different Lutheran groups and 14 denominations that all claim to be the Church of God.

The Brethren are not immune to division for they have eleven groups and the history of one of those groups (the Plymouth Brethren) is replete with division after division. During the last

150 years we have seen the Open Brethren, the Hopkins Brethren, the Needed Truth Brethren, the Luxmore Needed Truth Brethren, the Vernal Needed Truth Brethren, the Grant Brethren, the Kelly Brethren, Stuart Exclusives, Lowe Exclusives, Stoney Exclusives, Taylor Exclusives . . .

And if you have seen Garrisons Keillor's *Lake Wobegon Days*, you will read an entertaining yet sad chapter about his early days growing up in the Brethren movement. He tells of the Cox Brethren, Johnson Brethren, Dennis Brethren, Bud Brethren and the Beale, or Cold Water, Brethren.

The Church of Jesus Christ is hopelessly divided into hundreds of groups that believe different doctrines, practice different rites and ceremonies, and argue over major and minor issues.

Yet, Jesus, in his High Priestly prayer in John 17, said:

'I pray that they may be one as we are one' (verse 11).

'I pray that all of them may be one, Father, just as you are in me and I am in you' (verse 21).

'I have given them the glory that you gave me, that they may be one as we are one' (verse 22).

'May they be brought to complete unity to let the world know that you sent me and have loved them even as you loved me' (verse 23).

What lofty goals the Lord Jesus had. Yet, we have so miserably failed. I wonder what he thinks as he looks down and sees such a plethora of divisions among us today.

In Ephesians 4, Paul emphasizes the spiritual, organic unity— the one body, one spirit, one hope, one Lord, one faith, one baptism, one God and Father of all. (Ephesians 4:4–6). Then he proceeds to talk about another kind of unity. He says:

When Christ ascended higher than the heavens, he gave gifts— apostles, prophets, evangelists, pastor/teachers—to the church, to prepare God's people for works of service so that the body of Christ may be built up until we all reach *unity in the faith* and in the knowledge of the Son of God *and become mature*, attaining to the whole measure of the fullness of Christ.

Then we will no longer be infants tossed back and forth by the waves, and blown here and there by every wind of teaching and by the cunning and craftiness of men in their deceitful scheming. Instead, speaking the truth in love, we will in all things grow up into Him who is the Head, that is Christ. From Him the whole body, joined and held together by every supporting ligament, grows and builds itself up in love, as each part does its work. (Ephesians 4:12–16).

Dr. David Hesselgrave, professor of Missions at Trinity Seminary, says the unity that Christ prayed for was: 'the visible unity of Christian maturity which is expressed in upbuilding service, doctrinal knowledge, and mutual love in churches wherever they are found around the world.'

It is in the areas of *life, love, service* and *belief* that Christ longs that we be one.

1. Unity of Life

Unity of life is primarily what Jesus is talking about in John 17. The oneness our Lord asked for is not affected by the shattering of Christendom into 10,000 fragments. It is divine operation in which human action plays no part and which diversity of background, tradition, outlook, custom, form or prejudice cannot touch.

Jesus is talking about a body with its living members. 'As the body is one and has many members, and all the members being many are one body, so also is Christ.' Common life pervades the Father and the Son, and common life pervades the one body with its many members.

Jesus prayed that 'they may be one even as we are one.' How are the Father and Son one? In some pact or agreement or alliance, held together by a written document or on certain beliefs? No, not at all. They are one in Spirit, in nature, in essence, in life!

Ray Stedman says: 'The church is not to be a conglomeration of individuals who happen to agree upon certain ideas. It is bound together as an organism in a bodily unit. It is true that a body is an organization, but it is much more than an organization. The essence of the body is that it consists of thousands of cells with one mutually shared life.

'Contrary to the old song, a body is not produced by combining sections of anatomy together, by the toe bone being joined

to the foot bone and the foot bone to the ankle bone and the
ankle bone to the leg bone, etc. A body is formed by the
extension of one original cell which grows until it becomes a
mature body in which every cell shares the original life of the
original cell. That is the secret of a body—all parts of it share
life together.'

Race, colour, temperament, beliefs, or practices are not the
issue. It is the common life of Christ flowing through us that
gives us an essential unity and binds the body together.

Included in the one body are Catholics and charismatics,
Russians and Americans, blacks and whites, children and octo-
genarians. If they have accepted Jesus Christ as their personal
Saviour, they are a part of the family of God. We are all intrinsically
united together and we cannot, and we must not, deny or reject
that unity in the body. If we do, we have violated Scripture,
denied the unity between Father and Son, and rejected the heart
cry of Jesus our Saviour in his High Priestly prayer.

When Jesus cried out in prayer that we may be one as he and
the Father were one, it was this unity of life that he knew would
bind his body on earth together. It could only come about
through his shed blood on the cross. He knew that, and that
was part of the anguish he felt as he looked forward to the time
when he would lay down his life for the Church.

2. Unity of Love

Jesus not only had in mind a unity of life when he prayed the
prayer in John 17, but also a unity of love.

The unity of love exists eternally between the Father and the
Son. There is no way that the Father could not love the Son.
Nor could the Son ever not love the Father. There was an eternal
reality about the love that existed between the two.

And Jesus, as he is praying, thinks about the divisions that
would come because of a lack of love between his followers. So
in the agony of his prayer there is also an urgency that comes
from the Saviour: 'O Father, I want them to be one like we are
one.' I want love to permeate the lives of my followers, he says,
so that they will be like us.

Verse 23 says that 'the world will know you have sent me, and
have loved them as you have loved me', when they see the unity

of the body of Christ. They will know we are Christians by our love.

If the Father is in Christ, and Christ is in us, then the Father is in us and we are drawn into the very life of God, and the life of God is perfect in love. It is in loving one another that the oneness of all believers comes into full expression.

Yet, we so often see a lack of genuine love among brothers and sisters in Christ, and we see it lacking between churches and denominational groups.

Not only should our love for each other be a demonstration of our unity, but it is also an example to the world around us.

Tragically we are often guilty of gossip, defamation of character, innuendo, harsh words, and a lack of trust of one another. The world knows it and our testimony is ruined because of bitterness, rivalry, argument, hatred, competition and ill feeling. This is diametrically opposite to what Jesus wanted and that for which he prayed. He prayed that we would be known by our love.

The world should see us as a warm, loving, forgiving, gracious, caring, accepting community. If they did, they would rush to join us and our churches would be packed to the doors because we were known for our love for one another.

Someone has written all too truthfully:

To live above with saints we love,
O that will be glory,
But to live below with saints we know,
Now that's a different story.

3. Unity of Service

Ephesians 4 speaks of 'the whole body joined and held together by every supporting ligament, growing and building itself up in love as each part does its work.'

This is a picture of the unity of service both at the local church level and also at the Church Universal level. There must be a unified demonstration of service with all members of the body knowing their spiritual gifts and using them to the maximum capacity.

True unity will not take place until each one of us knows our part and plays it with all of our might. There is an enormous breakdown in this area. At the local church level we are negligent at developing people's gifts and organizing their use into an effective system. We are unnecessarily afraid of too much organization in service ministries.

The local church needs a systematic plan of ministries which builds the local body of Christ, and impacts the community with works of love that draw people to our Saviour the Lord Jesus.

Many churches are also not sure how to treat para-church organizations and their broad service impact upon the world. We should see them as a part of the body of Christ universal, reaching out in ways that local churches can not. We should be supportive in personnel and money so that the works of service might be expanded and enlarged beyond our local church horizons.

In addition, we need to see cooperative church programmes that would help local churches with growth and change. There should be creative ideas for television, radio, street theatre, drama, etc., that could be used by local churches for evangelism outreach and community impact. In a structure such as ours, we suffer from a lack of community presence. Local churches in the same area could unite for advertising, cooperation and encouragement of one another. This unified service idea could enhance the life and outreach of many churches.

Unity in service is so desperately needed among us. We could have such a greater local, national and world-wide impact if there was unity in service with members of the body cooperating, and building together for the progress of the Church of Jesus Christ throughout the world.

There is a fourth area of unity that is by far the most difficult. It is:

4. Unity of Belief

Now there are certain truths which I call FUNDAMENTALS, which are critical to the Christian faith. We must maintain unity in these areas. There are also some DISTINCTIVES which we adhere to, and then there are SECONDARY ISSUES. Let's look at these three areas.

A. FUNDAMENTALS

I believe they are:
1. *The Trinity*—there is one God eternally existing in three persons.
2. *The Inspiration of Scripture.* The Bible is truly the Word of God.
3. *The Deity of Christ.* The Lord Jesus is absolutely God.
4. *The Incarnation.* Jesus Christ is also perfect Man.
5. *The substitutionary death of Christ on the cross, his burial, resurrection and ascension into Heaven.*
6. *Salvation is by grace through faith and apart from works.*
7. *Jesus Christ will return.*
8. *The eternal punishment of the lost and the eternal joy of the redeemed.*

These fundamentals are clearly taught in Scripture and they are not negotiable. We must have unity on these doctrines. This is the irreducible minimum for which we must be willing to die.

There is a second group of teachings that I call:

B. DISTINCTIVES

These distinguish us from others. They do not irreparably separate us from other members of the body, but they are distinctives for which we are known. We believe they are important.

These distinctives primarily relate to our ecclesiology:

1. *Multiple Eldership*—We believe each local church should have as its primary authority a group of godly elders who set the agenda and watch over the spiritual life of the members.
2. *Autonomy of the Local Church*—We believe that each individual church has its own authority and should not be subjected to a higher authority of control apart from Christ himself. There certainly should be fellowship of churches to encourage and strengthen each other because autonomy is not the same as independence. We must maintain autonomy, but we do not have to be independent. Legislation and control from outside sources should be repudiated

and resisted. But we do need challenge, encouragement, assistance and practical help. We are in serious danger today of becoming cultic about independence. Our heritage has given us an unbalanced position that isolates, and results in weak churches trying to survive on their own.

The biggest impediment to unity is independence. We need to be strict on autonomy but not independence. Local churches need to feel that they are a part of a cause bigger than their own services or ministries. It is all too easy for a local church to be isolated in its own independency.

Loneliness is a form of sickness—in humans and in churches. Uniting in fellowship protects us from this sickness. Cooperation in mission is in harmony with the purposes of God.

I believe the balance is AUTONOMY and INTER-DEPENDENCE. We have seriously confused this issue and as a result we have lost balance.

3. *Open Communion*—We believe in a regular time of remembrance of the Lord's death, burial and resurrection.

During this time the priesthood of believers can be expressed publicly, and members of the body of Christ, who are in fellowship with the Lord, can share together their common life and love for the Lord in worship, praise, prayer and thanksgiving.

Now beyond the fundamentals and distinctives are all kinds of issues that divide and disturb the body of Christ. These I call:

C. SECONDARY ISSUES

By secondary issues I do not mean they are unimportant. They *are* important, but we must allow for differences of opinion without divisiveness.

On these issues we must be willing to demonstrate our love for those who differ with us. We *cannot* divide and destroy churches over secondary issues.

Enforced uniformity on secondary issues has been tried to secure the unity of believers and it doesn't work. The freedom granted to us in Christ is destroyed when we try to force uniformity in nonessentials.

You can tie two cats' tails together and hang them over a fence and you may have uniformity but you do not have unity. One cannot do better than quote from the famous epigram attributed to Rupert Meldonius and quoted by Richard Baxter:

'In essentials, unity; in nonessentials, liberty; in all things, charity.'

David Lloyd George, the former Prime Minister of England, was a member of a small independent church. He once said, 'The church I belong to is in a fierce dispute. One faction says that baptism is *in* the name of Christ, and the other that it is *into* the name of Christ. I belong to one of these parties. I feel most strongly about it. I would die for it in fact, but I forget which it is.'

Some secondary issues are:

- Bible versions
- Wine or grape juice at the Lord's Supper
- Making financial needs known
- Women's head coverings
- Women's participation in public service
- Divorce and remarriage
- The sign gifts
- Prophecy
- Type of music permitted
- Full-time workers in a local church
- Regular financial support to full-time workers
- Five point Calvinism
- Associations with other evangelicals

A hundred other issues could be listed.

Each local church should discuss these issues and decide their position. No one has the right or authority to tell the autonomous local church what it should or should not believe on these issues.

Neither should one local church force its decisions upon another. Local churches with different perspectives on these matters should be able to fellowship in harmony with one another, demonstrating the unity of the Body of Christ.

We must allow for divergent positions on these matters. Threatening or suggesting that some should leave if they do not practice the same as we do, or as was traditionally a part of our movement, is a denial of the autonomy of the local church and the unity of the Body of Christ.

We must have a wide view that is inclusive rather than exclusive.

Someone has written:

He drew a circle that shut me out,
Heretic, rebel, a thing to flout.
But love and I had the wit to win,
We drew a circle that took him in.

We must be committed to drawing a large circle—we must not reject our brothers and sisters because of secondary issues.

Churches can and should be different in secondary matters. Wouldn't it be a testimony to the grace of God if we could have a movement of autonomous churches—completely unified on the essential doctrines, but allowing each local church to decide the secondary issues, so that there was a broad spectrum of colour and sound . . . really showing the world that we can differ on non-essentials and be united together to encourage and help one another.

This is the practical truth of the unity of the body of Christ—autonomous and interdependent, unity on fundamentals, and diversity on secondary issues.

If ever there is an hour, it is now to pull together groups of churches on a national or regional basis to help one another become the churches we should be. There should be a single vision for glorifying our Lord Jesus and growing spiritually and numerically. We must set aside unfounded fears of denomination-alism and aggressively plan and work for a unity that causes us to see churches flourishing.

It will take men and women with big hearts to avoid gettin tied up on the nonessentials, but to see the enormous possibilities if we are willing to work for growth.

Let's get rid of sectarianism. Let's get rid of criticism. Let's get rid of negativism and let's unite in a positive, forward moving force that will enable all of us to be dynamic witnesses to God's power in our times.

We don't need more divisions over secondary issues. We need to accept one another and earnestly endeavour to keep the unity of the Spirit in the bond of peace.

Let us accept those who are more conservative than we are.

Let us accept those who have a more progressive position than we do.

Let us be known because of our love for one another and our ability to allow each local church to decide its own issues and be what it wants to be without interference from others. Then we will truly have a fellowship of autonomous churches with unity in the body of Christ, and the differences at the local church level.

Why can't we live and work with such a position?

Harold St. John, the great assembly Bible teacher in England of a generation ago, said, 'There must be great breadth of charity and wide divergence in local assemblies. Difference may exist without breach of fellowship.' And I heartily concur.

The story is told of a preacher who was visiting a seaside resort area. One day he went for a walk along the beach. The tide was unusually low that day. At one spot he came upon several acres of exposed brown rock. Carefully, he picked his way over this jagged surface to examine more closely the exposed formation. The entire area was pock-marked with small pools that swarmed with tiny marine life. Stooping down, he began to interview the little creatures.

'How long have you been living here?' he asked.

'Oh, for a long time, ever since the tide went out,' replied one.

'Well, I see that you are not alone. You have plenty of neighbours just like you. Why, there's a pothole full of them right next to you here.'

'But we have nothing whatever to do with them!' snapped one wiggler. 'Those people left us, you know. We used to be all together, but they got mad and broke away when the tide went out.'

'That's really too bad,' the preacher observed. 'They look like you. They behave like you and probably like the same foods. In fact, I can't see any difference between you and them at all.'

'Oh, but there is a difference. They are extremely shallow fellows and really have no depth at all.'

'What do you mean?'

'Well, look for yourself. Their pothole is only seven inches deep.'

'And how deep is yours?' the preacher inquired.

'Ours? Why, ours is 8½ inches! In fact, we have one spot that is over nine.'

'But let me tell you something else. Those people are quite narrow too.'

'Narrow?'

'Sure. Their pool is only ten inches wide. Ours is eleven and a quarter.' The little swimmer swelled up as he made this significant pronouncement.

The preacher's curiosity was now unrestrained. He chanced one more question.

'Say, what do you call your . . . your place here?'

'This, sir,' and now he really did expand, 'is the Atlantic Ocean.'

The preacher picked his way back over the rocks.

High tide came in six hours later. Those acres of potholes were completely covered and all those little creatures were swimming together again.

The preacher cried, 'Lord, send in the tide today!'

There is a *unity of life*, a *unity of love*, a *unity of service*, and a *unity of belief*. Within the unity of belief area there are non-negotiables and there are negotiables.

Let's fight for the non-negotiables, but let us allow for differences within the area of the negotiables so that we are bound together, not by the negatives of secondary issues, but by the positives of our love and life in Christ.

And let the tide come in so that all of us are swimming together in the great ocean of God's love, with a unity that shows the world that we are Christ's.

Questions for Discussion

Biblical

1. Do you agree with this chapter that unity needs to be demonstrated in *life*, *love*, *service* and *belief*? Can you rank these four things in an order of importance?

2. Sometimes we *have* to separate ourselves from Christian brothers and sisters for good reasons (see e.g. Rom 16:17, Titus

3:10, 1 Cor 5:11). What are the biblical reasons for separation? And what possible reasons for separation does the Bible *not* condone?

3. This chapter draws a distinction between different types of convictions—'fundamentals', 'distinctives' and 'secondary issues'. How do we decide which is which? Do you agree with Kevin Dyer's list of 'fundamentals' and Brethren 'distinctives'?

Practical

1. What can we do about Christians who plainly do not want to be in very close unity with us?

2. 'True unity will not take place until each one of us knows our part and does it with all of our might. There is a tremendous breakdown in this area.' How can a local church structure itself in such a way that all members *are* fulfilling their role effectively and enthusiastically?

3. 'The biggest impediment to unity is independence . . . Local churches need to feel that they are part of a cause bigger than their own services or ministries.' Do you agree? How do we set the balance right?

Action

1. 'If ever there is an hour, it is now, to pull together groups of churches on a national or regional basis to help one another become the churches we should be.' How could this happen in your part of the world? Has it started? If so, how effective is your church's support for the moves which are being made? If *not*, what part could you play in starting things happening?

2. What relationship does your church have with (a) other churches in your area (b) churches from a similar denominational background throughout the country? is there room for improvement? What could you practically do?

3. Are there attitudes which need to be changed in your church, if true unity is to be a reality? How can you begin to alter people's perspectives?

Chapter 2

Organizing Leadership for Effective Ministry

THROUGH the years many people have taken strong positions on the question of church leadership. Some have fought for one-man leadership while others have repudiated it in favour of a multiple-elder structure.

In some churches, regardless of their insistence on a plurality of elders, one man does all the decision making, not because he is gifted in leadership, but because he is the oldest or has the strongest, most dogmatic personality. Although this passes for plurality of leadership, the other elders serve as rubber stamps to the one man.

In other churches where more than one strong or dogmatic person exists among the elders, everyone tries to do everything and the result is in-fighting which depletes the strength of the church so that little or no vision or direction can emerge.

Other churches suffer from an almost total lack of leadership. The doors are opened regularly, services are held, but there is essentially no plan or direction in place. Basically no one leads beyond the essentials of keeping the building functional and the pulpit filled.

In a few places it is the wives who have a controlling influence. The subtle power of the wives behind the elders is the real issue to reckon with.

In many places there is a real fear of leadership. Anyone who begins to move forward as a leader threatens the 'position' of the elders who do not have the same leadership ability. Therefore, they put him down on the charge that he is trying to 'take over.'

While not all churches have leadership problems as severe as those I have listed, I believe we all need to rethink our pre-suppositions concerning leadership.

There are three important issues for us to consider:

1) The difference between eldership and leadership.
2) The qualities of leadership that are demanded.
3) The responsibilities of leadership that are required.

The Difference between Eldership and Leadership

I grew up in a church that had great warmth and love. There was vision and vitality. The young men were encouraged to participate in the meetings. Even when we were just boys we were asked to read the Scriptures, quote a verse or pray. There was vision, vitality, outreach, growth, warmth, and love, but there was a serious misunderstanding about leadership.

Our church didn't have elders. Instead, each month a business meeting was held when all the key men were invited to discuss the affairs of the church. Among this group were some godly elders. They were real shepherds of the flock. They were compassionate and caring. They ministered to the needs of the people. Also in this group were one or two men with outstanding leadership ability.

Most of the men were farmers, factory workers, labourers and shopkeepers. They came together at night and tried to become administrators. I watched as farmers with warped ideas of what it means to be a leader became very powerful in the church. They were used to bossing the cows about the farmyard, and they carried some of those ideas over into the church.

Most of the men never practised leadership in their jobs and they were expected to be transformed by a change of clothes when they attended the business meeting at night. It didn't work, and I could sense the ineptness of the whole situation.

I had no idea then that it was not biblical either. What had happened was that my home church had been strongly influenced by John Nelson Darby's ecclesiology which taught that the church was in ruin and, therefore, the offices of elder and deacon were no longer valid.

Unfortunately, many British churches were also influenced by Darby's teaching even though they repudiated his exclusivism. As a result, there are very few of our churches today that have a functioning deacon group and there are still hundreds of churches without a clearly defined understanding of the difference between eldership and leadership.

Many elders today don't know how to lead. They assume leadership is a *position* when in fact it is a *function*. Eldership is a position based on an active modelling role whereas leadership is a gift, an ability to function in leading. Not all elders are leaders, nor are they meant to be. Until we clearly distinguish in our minds this critical difference, we will not see dramatic growth and vibrancy in our churches.

Eldership is an office, and those who meet the requirements of 1 Timothy 3 and other passages should take that position when recognized by the body.

Leadership, on the other hand, is a gift given sovereignly by the Holy Spirit to whomever he chooses. And those with this gift should function in the church under the direction of the elders.

The biblical qualifications for elders mostly relate to personal character qualities, while only a few are functional qualities. They primarily have to do with the character and life of the elder.

He must be above reproach, the husband of one wife, temperate, self-controlled, respectable, hospitable, apt to teach, not given to much wine, not violent but gentle, not quarrelsome, not a lover of money, able to manage his family well and see that his children obey him, not a recent convert, and he must have a good reputation.

Eldership should not be based on gift but on a modelling of spiritual life. But we have taken the multiple eldership truth and mixed it with a non-biblical idea of multiple leadership.

We have done this to preserve our distinctive of not having one-man leadership. Historically it grew out of our repudiation of the error of dominant one-man control in the Church of England and the Roman Catholic Church which the early Brethren left.

However, they went too far, and came up with a multiple leadership structure (which is not biblical) instead of a multiple eldership structure (which is biblical).

Let me re-emphasize, eldership is an office; leadership is a gift, and today we must recognize leadership and allow it to function in the body.

Elders establish a quality of life in the church. Leaders give vision and direction to that life so it will infuse the people and the body will grow both quantitatively and qualitatively.

In some cases the person or persons with the clear gift of leadership may also hold the office of eldership. But we must let the elders rule and let the leaders lead.

The early Brethren reacted so strongly that they led us into a non-biblical pattern that is thwarting growth and resulting in impotency among churches today. The gifts of leader, administrator and pastor/teacher have all been down-played in our circles to the detriment of our church life and growth.

We are reaping today a harvest of ineffectiveness as a result of 150 years of confusion about elder rule and leadership responsibility.

All elders have spiritual gifts—but not all elders have the gift of leadership, or the gift of administration, or the gift of pastor/ teacher. The Spirit gave '*some*' these gifts. All elders are equal in terms of their office. They are not equal in terms of gift. A few will have high visibility, others will function in the background.

Take the 12 disciples for a moment. All were equal in terms of their office and privilege. There are four lists in the New Testament of the disciples' names. Peter, James, John and Andrew are always listed first in all accounts and Peter is always the number one name. He became the spokesman for the entire group. They had equal honour, equal office, equal privilege, equal responsibility. They were all sent out two by two. They all preached the Kingdom. They all healed. They all had access to Jesus.

But while none of them was less than the others in terms of office and spiritual qualifications (except Judas), nevertheless, some stood out over the others as leaders. Peter as the spokesman was dominant and he gave special leadership to the group.

The same phenomenon can be observed in the book of Acts. James, for example, was regarded as a leader and spokesman for the entire church (Acts 12:17, 15:13–21). Although he was not in any kind of official position over the elders, they recognized his gift of leadership and looked to him for that.

Peter and John were the two main characters of the first 12

chapters of Acts. Yet there is no record that John ever preached a single sermon. Peter did all the talking. He was the spokesman. John's was a support role, not a less important role but a different one. Peter had the unique gift of leadership and in the plan of God he was the leader and spokesman.

In the sovereignty of God the emphasis moved to Antioch. Barnabas came from Jerusalem to see what was happening. He went to Tarsus and got Paul and they spent a year in Antioch and 'became leaders of the church there.'

Beginning in Acts 13, Paul and Barnabas become the dominant characters. Although Barnabas was probably one of the leading teachers in the church before Paul came in, he soon became less visible and his messages are not recorded. Paul became the obvious leader. Barnabas was no less important but he had a different role.

In Acts 15:22 we read:

> 'The apostles and elders with the whole church decided to choose some of their own men and send them to Antioch with Paul and Barnabas. They chose Judas and Silas, two men who were leaders among the brothers.'

So we must recognize multiple eldership and we must recognize the gift of leadership. Obviously those with the gift of leadership must be accountable to the elders.

This prevents the emergence of independent self-styled leadership, with no accountability, from dominating the local church (like Diotrephes 'who loves to be first'—3 John 9).

Let us take a few moments to try to define some terms.

First for the elders, there are three words used in the New Testament.

ELDER (*presbyteros*): literally speaks of individuals who are older and who in biblical culture had earned respect by virtue of their character, experience and years.

BISHOP (*episkopos*): speaks of individuals who oversee, take care of people and visit. The picture is that of a very person-oriented individual who stays in close touch with and cares for others.

PASTOR (*poimen*): is literally 'shepherd'. It focuses attention on close relationships and care for the growth and well being of members of the body.

None of these words for elder, bishop or pastor suggest they are managers of an enterprise or decision makers, but rather they speak of one who, with the wisdom gained by personal experience, builds an intimate relationship with others whom he cares for and tends with a view toward growth and maturity.

It's the care of the members with which the elders must concern themselves, not the management of the body. That is a leader's role.
Secondly, the word . . .

LEADERSHIP (*proistemi*): Romans 12:8—'If it is leadership, let him govern diligently.' Literally means 'to stand before', to lead, to attend to.

ADMINISTRATION (*kubernesis*): 1 Corinthians 12:28—'those with gifts of administration'; literally means *helmsman, captain of a ship, one who steers a boat.*

Often a person with the gift of leadership also has the gift of administration. However, in other people the gift of leadership is combined with a variety of gifts. A clear, distinct understanding of the differences between eldership and leadership will help us immeasurably to allow leadership to rise to the top and function so that our churches can be renewed and grow.

It must also be remembered that while there probably will be one primary leader who encapsulates the vision, there will also be subordinate leaders in different aspects of the ministry.

It is interesting to note that most of the growing, dynamic, large churches in both the U.S. and Canada have faced up to this question so that the elders rule and the leaders lead. There are clearly defined public leaders whom people obviously look to as the primary leadership person.

Public leaders should not have unbridled control. They must be accountable to multiple eldership and they must be given the freedom to be the leader God gifted them to be. Style will differ, complementary gifts will differ, but if those with the gift of leadership are set free to use their God-given gift, we will have dynamic, growing churches.

Sometimes leadership is combined with the gifts of administrator or prophet (1 Corinthians 14:3 style) or pastor/teacher or evangelist. Whatever the combination, leadership is recognized and is allowed to function so that the body is given direction and every member can become an active member under the leadership of those God has gifted for that function.

Now I want to discuss briefly the qualities of leadership and the responsibilities of leadership.

The qualities of leadership that are demanded

Leadership is not a title that grants you the license to force others to knuckle under. It is a skill you perform, a service you render for the whole church. Some qualities of leadership include:

1) A special anointing of the Holy Spirit

Leadership is a gift of the Holy Spirit. A lot of elders and full-time workers are trying to be leaders when they don't have the gift. One of the toughest questions you can ask yourself is, 'Am I occupying a place of leadership without the gift from the Holy Spirit?'

It would relieve a great deal of stress among elders if we could honestly face up to the issue and recognize those who really have the gift and those who don't.

This doesn't mean getting out of ministry or not functioning as an elder, but it does mean getting a realistic evaluation of your gifts and having a significant ministry within the limits of those gifts apart from leadership.

2) Vision

The leader is the custodian of the vision of the church. The ownership belongs to the elders but communication of it to the flock is the responsibility of the leader.

Some communicate the vision through the additional gift of preaching or teaching, others through the gift of administration, and so on.

3) Sensitivity to people

The leader must be sensitive to the flock. He listens, he evaluates, he cares. He is committed to service.

4) Self knowledge

The leader knows himself. He knows his own strengths and weaknesses. He must learn to persevere. He must go on when the going is rough. He is not a quitter. He must be disciplined. An undisciplined leader is no leader at all.

Those who can't control their time, energies and appetites have negated their leadership. Leaders must be able to meet deadlines. They must be responsible in time management and administration.

5) A strong spiritual centre

It has been said that this is the number one problem among leaders today. They live on the spiritual edge. If you and I expect to be true leaders, then our spiritual centre must be strong so that Satan doesn't drain us and wean us away. We must have mastered our own weakness by the power of the Holy Spirit.

6) Ability to prioritize

Unless leaders can control and master their schedules successfully and accomplish goals and objectives, then they are not real leaders. Many with the gift of pastor/teacher are not leaders because they cannot control events—events control them.

7) Ability to confront

A leader is able to face up to issues and deal with them. He doesn't push things under the rug and hope they will go away. A true leader confronts with kindness and firmness.

One of the most popular concepts today is servant leadership. Properly understood it is a helpful concept, but it has been terribly abused.

The Christian leader is primarily a servant of God, not a servant of the sheep. Many leaders act as if they are servants of the sheep, which is a faulty concept. The leader is a servant of God, given to absolute obedience to him and to what he says. To extend that, and say you are the servant of each sheep, is a fallacy.

Lee Iacocca is a great leader in industry. He is the servant of the Chrysler Corporation but he doesn't ask the assembly line worker to decide where the company should go. He may solicit opinions, but he asks the man on the machine only to run the machine and run it well . . . and have faith in the company.

Iaccoca's servanthood is expressed by his leadership. There are leaders who constantly ask the sheep which way to go. If the leader quits leading the sheep and starts following them, he is no longer a trustworthy leader.

If my gift is leading (as evidenced by my having followers), then my serving is leading.

Leadership can be coached but never implanted. You can't make a leader out of someone without an innate gift of leadership. If a person has innate ability, circumstances and training will bring it out.

The responsibilities of leadership that are required

Broadly speaking the responsibility of leadership is to bring people together in order to accomplish common goals. A true leader is committed to the cause—he does not become the cause.

Many leaders seek to build people around themselves. This is faulty leadership. It is leadership that deprecates the truth of the unity of the body of Christ.

A leader's job is to arouse the various constituent elements of the church in a Spirit-filled call to forward God's mission in the area.

Unfortunately when we have 'leaders' who don't have the gift of leadership, we stagnate or become divisive or maintain the *status quo*.

The primary responsibilities of leadership are:

1) Maintain the Vision

The leader's number one job is to articulate, maintain, and develop the church's purpose and goals. He needs to be able to define the vision specifically and give it a single focus. He must be able to communicate it effectively to others and he must persuade the people in the fellowship personally to accept the vision. And he must persist by repeating it over and over again. Until the church is willing to accept the vision and be a part of it, there will be little growth.

2) Gather Others around the Vision

The true leader coagulates followers around the vision, not around himself. The leader does not generally attract people to the vision with emotion but with comprehension.

Therefore, he must be a communicator of information; persuasion is greatly enhanced by comprehension. The more information given to the people, the better.

3) Know the Value of Organization

The value of management and administration is inestimable in the effective church. Many small churches have no management of their functions. Don't forget, you lead people but you manage work. There is a tremendous amount of work going on that could be so much more effective if it were managed properly.

4) Learn to Delegate

The leader recognizes he can't do all the work himself and he parcels it out to responsible people whom he holds accountable.

A.T. Cushman, the Chief Executive Officer of Sears, said, 'The art of administration is constantly checking.' You must check up on what is happening. The leader who refuses to follow through with those to whom he has delegated responsibility has abdicated his leadership role.

5) Establish Communication

Those who are directly accountable to the leader must have clear communication channels and they must learn to communicate to those for whom they are responsible.

6) Anticipate Problems

The leader tries to resolve problems before they get out of hand. He never allows uprisings or hurt feelings to develop but quietly goes around putting out fires and encouraging whole-hearted participation in the vision.

The true leader has many other burdens to bear. He is a motivator, a goal setter, a controller, a trainer, a director, a planner, an evaluator, an influencer and a supervisor.

In our circles we are very much afraid of organization. We have for years bought into the philosophy that the church is an organism and not an organization. That is a half truth. Organisms have organization. The New Testament church has both dimensions. It is both an organism and an organization.

We traditionally have espoused the organism concept but have been desperately lacking on the organizational end. One of the prime functions of leadership is to make all the resources of the body of Christ available to everyone. He becomes the networker, the facilitator, helping people turn to one another, recognizing gifts and resources within the body.

In summary, I believe we are suffering today because of a variety of misconceptions and fears.

We are afraid of allowing leadership to surface because we are so committed to multiple leadership instead of multiple eldership.

We are afraid of one man ministry and so we fight any attempt to allow men of special gift to rise and be recognized.

We are afraid of recognizing the various gifts the Holy Spirit has given to the church because of the so-called charismatic gifts. As a result we have downgraded the use of various gifts— including leadership.

We are afraid of allowing national models to develop who impact the churches at large because of our fear of control. We have an irrational concern that someone might want to control and dictate so that the autonomy of the local church would be lost.

What we urgently need is a fresh vision of the Church, a new vibrancy of the Holy Spirit's power, a release from our inordinate fears, a positive marching forward with Christ as the Head of the Church, functioning elders who care for the flock, recognized leaders who lead and administer the body, and the use of the gifts Christ has given to the Church for its edification.

Questions for Discussion

Biblical

1. Look at the Scriptures which talk about the responsibilities of eldership (e.g. Acts 20:17–35, 1 Tim 3:1–7, Titus 1:5–9, 1 Pet 5:1–4). Do you agree that 'eldership is a position based on an active modelling role . . . Not all elders are leaders, nor are they meant to be'?

2. Three verses in the New Testament use the key word *proistemi*, mentioned by this chapter, to talk about leadership. They are Rom 12:8, 1 Thessalonians 5:8, and 1 Tim 5:17. Read them and list what they tell you about the responsibilities of leaders and followers to one another.

3. Look at the qualities of leadership listed in this chapter. Can you think of biblical examples of each? Can you think of other biblical qualities of leadership which you would add to this list?

Practical

1. Can you think of examples of churches known to you where the functions of *eldership* and *leadership* are distinguished, in the way described in this chapter?

2. 'We are reaping today a harvest of ineffectiveness as a result of 150 years of confusion about elder rule and leadership responsibility.' Is this true?

3. 'We are afraid of one man ministry so we fight any attempt to allow men of special gift to rise and be recognized.' Would you agree? Could this be why so many gifted Brethren have achieved prominence in para-church movements (and other churches) rather than their own local church?

Action

1. Is your church structured in such a way that the leaders can lead and the elders can rule? If not, what changes would you have to make for this to happen?

2. How do you decide who is gifted for leadership within your church?

3. If leaders 'must be accountable to multiple eldership', how do you avoid frustration when non-leaders, who don't share the leaders' sense of vision and haven't been part of their discussions, rule against ideas which the leaders strongly wish to pursue? Could this be a problem in your church?

Chapter 3

The Agony of Change, the Ecstasy of Revival

CHUCK Swindoll tells a story about a fellow who was raised in the back hills of West Virginia. He lived so far out in the sticks that he had never even been to the big city nor seen modern inventions, flashing neon lights or the dazzle of city living.

He married a girl just like himself, and they spent all their married years in the backwoods. They had one son whom they had creatively named Junior. Around the time Junior reached his sixteenth birthday his Dad began to realize it wouldn't be too many years before his son would become a man and strike out on his own.

It troubled him that his boy could reach manhood, go to try to get a job in the city, and not be prepared to face the real world. So he started to save money for a trip the three of them would take to the city.

About three years later the big day arrived. They tossed their belongings in the old pick-up and started the long journey over winding, rough roads to the city. Their plan was to spend several days at a swanky hotel and take in all the sights.

As they approached the outskirts of the metropolis, Papa began to get a little jumpy.

'Mama, when we pull up at the hotel you stay in the truck while Junior and I go in and look around. We'll come back and get ya, okay?' She agreed.

Flashing neon signs and uniformed doormen greeted them as they pulled up. Mama stayed while Papa and Junior walked wide-eyed toward the lobby. Neither could believe their eyes. When they stepped on a mat the doors opened automatically. Inside they stood with their mouths wide open staring at the first chandelier either of them had ever seen. It hung from the ceiling three storeys high.

Off to the left was a waterfall rippling over inlaid stones and rocks. 'Junior, look.' Papa was pointing to a long mall where shoppers were going in and out of beautiful stores.

'Papa, look down there.' Down below was an ice skating rink—inside! While they both stood silently watching one breathtaking sight after another, they kept hearing a clicking sound behind them.

Papa finally turned around and saw this amazing little room with doors that slid open at the centre. What in the world was that? People would walk up, push a button and wait. Lights would flicker above the doors and then, click, the doors would slide open from the middle.

Some people would walk inside and turn around as—click!— the doors slid shut. By now Papa and Junior stood totally transfixed.

At that moment a wrinkled old lady shuffled up to the doors all by herself. She pushed the button and waited a few seconds. The doors opened with a swish, and she hobbled into the little room. No one else stepped in with her, so—click!—the doors slid shut. Not more than thirty seconds later the doors opened again—and there stood this fabulous, attractive, blonde young woman in her twenties. High heels, shapely body, beautiful face—a real knock-out. As she stepped out, smiled and turned to walk away, Papa nudged his boy and mumbled, 'Hey, Junior . . . go get Mama.'

Now we all wish there was a machine like that to bring about such dramatic change, but unfortunately the reality is that change is very difficult to initiate, extremely hard to process and almost impossible to complete.

Very few people really want change. We are comfortable the way we are.

But it is imperative that we face up to this issue of change for even a vital, growing church is never free from decay and often needs to make changes. Unless we are very careful, we can be lulled to sleep until it is almost too late to make the changes we should.

Now we must remember that change is not always a good thing. Death is a form of change, so is deterioration. So it is not change just for the sake of change . . . it is change that is planned, prayed over and initiated carefully in a godly environment that is best.

Supermarkets have changed over the years. When I was a boy there were the mom-and-pop grocery stores where friendly relations, time and personal interest made shopping a joy.

In those days there were just a few hundred different items to purchase. The homespun grocery store was open from 9 a.m. to 5 p.m. Now supermarkets are open 24 hours a day. Today the average supermarket has 24,000 different products.

We have computerized voices at the cash register calling out the prices. You can find salt-free sections, sugar-free sections, Asian products, Spanish foods, and in America Wal-Mart is starting new supermarkets that provide one-stop shopping for groceries, clothes, medicines, shoes, hardware and everything else you need—all in one single store.

But church goes on the same. Breaking of Bread at 11:00 and the Gospel Service at 6:30—it was, and is, and shall be, forever more. No one can fail to see in some segments of assembly life the dry rot produced by tradition, apathy, rigidity and spiritual emptiness.

If you are doing the same thing you were doing ten years ago, or even five years ago, something is wrong. Society has moved. People's needs have changed, and if the church hasn't moved to meet those needs, we have denied the vitality of God's work and the Holy Spirit's power in our generation.

Apathy and lowered motivation are the most widely noted characteristics of a church on the downward path. If most of the people in your assembly are not personally involved in ministry, then there is trouble ahead. If we falter, it will be because of a failure of heart and spirit. We have the resources, but do we have the will to change?

As churches age, vitality tends to diminish, flexibility gives way to rigidity, creativity fades and there is a loss of capacity to meet challenges. The church, as it grows older, accumulates habits, attitudes, and opinions, and these tend to make it a little less receptive to alternative ways of thinking and acting.

Most of us don't have the privilege of starting a new work. We are in churches that have been going for 10, 20, 50 or 100 years. We are caught in situations where tradition is rampant.

There are so many things that need to be changed, and we are not sure where to start. And perhaps we are not even sure if we should start.

But if we are going to experience the ecstasy of revival, then what we need is a framework which is comprised of a few basic principles that don't change and a process that is constantly changing. It is this that leadership must understand. The framework is stable; the process is fluid. Now the framework, in my judgement, is comprised of four elements.

First, multiple eldership. We are thoroughly committed to a plurality of elders who are responsible for the spiritual life of the body.

Second, the regular celebration of the Lord's supper. Whether it is daily, weekly, bi-weekly or monthly must not be an issue because we are convinced of the truth of the Scriptures, that 'whenever you eat this bread and drink this cup, you proclaim the Lord's death until he comes'. And we want to proclaim the Lord's death as often as possible.

Third, the autonomy of the local church. Each local church, before God, sets its own direction and should not be controlled or manipulated by any outside individuals or organizations.

Fourth, the priesthood of all believers. Each individual can come directly to the Lord without any human mediator, and because of this, people participate in open worship and praise to God.

Now we hold these principles very dear. But it is very important to remember that:

Principles won't work without power

Orthodoxy regarding the principles doesn't automatically bring a growing, spiritually powerful church. We desperately need to get the power back into the principles.

I have visited 600 churches in North America. They all believe the principles, but I have seen very few which are powerfully being used by the Holy Spirit. We have put the emphasis on the principles to the detriment of the power. We are great for truth but are woefully short of Holy Spirit unction.

The principles themselves do not cause spiritual life and power. It is the presence and activity of the Holy Spirit who breathes life into the principles and revolutionizes churches.

Strategy, church growth principles and renewal conferences are all good. But they won't do the job unless there is a spirit-filled body of believers united for the glory of God and the impacting of society around us.

I suggest to you today that our problem is not with principles, but it is with the lack of power of the Holy Spirit of God in our midst.

In most churches we are going through the motions. We are playing church. There is little evidence that God the Holy Spirit is doing much among us.

If he was working among us, we would have churches packed to the doors with people trying to get in. We would be seeing people coming to Christ on a regular basis, and we would find believers drooling with joy waiting to lap up the Word of God and live holy, godly lives honouring to the Lord Jesus Christ. As it has been said, people like to go to church where people like to go to church.

So let us not be fooled into the idea that holding the principles alone will glorify God and result in a thriving church. Principles without power are the death knell of churches, and we have hundreds of dead and dying churches which are holding tenaciously to the principles. They are spiralling downward on a course to demise. New Christians find many of our churches an ageing, tired and tarnished community of believers.

The Spirit comes to bring renewed energy, to present fresh challenge, to encourage change and to commission us for service in the world. Divested of such power our churches are becoming empty rooms, shallow graves, and lifeless bodies. When God's Spirit is in full control, he can take the principles we hold and make our churches powerful, worshipping, evangelizing, discipling communities where Christ is uplifted and believers strengthened and refreshed.

Now if the principles won't work without the power, I also believe that:

Programmes won't work without the right spiritual climate

The 'climate' of a church is probably the most important

factor in enhancing growth and bringing about change. There are five measurements you can take to see if you have the right climate. If you are not making progress in these five areas, then there is little hope of making programme changes and expecting to see the results that we want.

1. A Positive Atmosphere

The emphasis must be on what God can do, not on what we cannot do. There are always plenty of negative people walking about with their faith extinguishers trying to put out any potential spiritual awakening.

What is desperately needed to balance these are other people who practice a positive faith in their walk with God and in their relationship with others. And we need those with a positive spirit to outnumber the negative people.

We need people committed to build, not destroy; to praise, not condemn; to encourage, not criticize; to help, not hinder; to give, not wanting to receive; to serve, not to be served; to forgive, not to judge.

Do you have people who are eager to catch people doing something right and congratulate them rather than always looking for something wrong and attacking them?

Your church needs to be a place where challenges can be dreamed and accepted. If the elders have a stifling stranglehold of control, there is not the positive climate to free people for ministry.

The second characteristic of a right spiritual climate conducive to growth and change is:

2. A Commitment to Excellence

So many churches I know have made peace with mediocrity. They are content with substandard effort. They are satisfied with just getting by. No wonder we have problems in increasing our numbers.

Our goal must always be to be our best in every part of the ministry. The emphasis on excellence is nothing more than being consistent with the glory of God. God deserves the best in new sheets, sermons, music, ushering, Sunday School, the creche, and a hundred other details that we face.

If it becomes known that we are a quality operation, then our image is enhanced and our attractiveness to the community increases proportionately.

The third characteristic of a right spiritual climate is:

3. Trust

The elders and full-time workers must have the trust and confidence of the people. The burden in creating a climate of trust rests on the one wanting to be trusted; you earn it. The people know you are not going to end-run them. You can lose graciously on an idea and not seek other means to get your way. It means you never resort to underhanded means to accomplish your goals. Trust is an important part of building the climate in the fellowship.

4. Flexibility

The willingness to experiment, to innovate, and even to fail are a part of flexibility. You can learn to adapt to difficult situations and people.

Flexibility allows us to make changes and adapt traditional events to be more appealing to the culture around us. If there is no flexibility among the elders or in the minds and hearts of full-time workers or key leaders, then you have a serious problem.

Finally, the last characteristic of a right spiritual climate is:

5. A Servant Spirit

I have heard so many times people saying that they get nothing out of the services. Instead of asking what we can do for God, we have slipped into the terrible attitude of wondering what God can do for us.

Service and sacrifice are words not acceptable to many today. They want to come and get, and get, and get . . . instead of coming to give, and give, and give. Unfortunately this atmosphere has become so prevalent that we catch ourselves asking if people *want* to serve. And put that way, many choose not to, and so dies an important ingredient to growth and change.

A better way is to start with the assumption that God's people *will* serve. That is a given.

The question is not *if* people will serve, but *where and how* they will serve. That assumption and commitment to service is a necessary mind-set for growth and change.

These five ingredients—a positive atmosphere, a commitment to excellence, trust, flexibility and a servant spirit—are the essential ingredients that make up the aura around a growing church.

Once we are making significant progress in these areas, we can begin to talk about programme changes. If we don't see the climate around a church changing to such an atmosphere, then the serious question must be asked about whether you should continue there.

For twenty years I have counselled young people and full-time workers to not give up easily. I think that is right, but in recent years it has become much clearer to me that we cannot continue in situations that aren't developing the positive atmosphere to bring about change.

The Spirit of God is anxious for us to see growth, change and a spiritual awakening.

It comes as we yield to the Holy Spirit's power and demonstrate his work in our lives by seeing a positive attitude, excellence, trust, flexibility, and a servant spirit characterize us personally, and our churches corporately.

Now assuming you are making progress in these areas, let's talk about what needs changing and how to make those changes.

First, I must caution you to not try to ram through changes in the programme without first working on these other essential elements we have talked about. Many churches have tried programme changes, and they won't work alone. We must be in the right spirit, with the right atmosphere, and then programme changes will bring great results.

It is often agonizing to make these changes, but they will be the spark of spiritual revival that will bring ecstasy to the believers.

The Changes We Must Make

I would like to suggest there are six urgent changes that need to be made in most churches. I know the depth and breath of the changes will vary, but it seems to me, from visiting a broad spectrum of churches, that we all are suffering the same problems.
The first change we must make is:

1. Revitalize the Worship Meeting

I have sat in at least two and a half thousand Breaking of Bread services, and I think that it is fair to say that the great majority of them have been slow, cold, unimaginative services that give little worship or glory to the Lord.

Now I know that in our movement we are touching the most sacred part of our churches when we talk about the Breaking of Bread. It has been our hallmark for 160 years. It is what distinguishes us. But we have fallen into the trap of the routine and predictable, and the dynamic of fervent, joyful worship that lifts Christ up and brings joy to our hearts is missing.

In many large American churches today, 400–700 people attend the 11 o'clock service and only 25 percent of that number go to the Breaking of Bread. Young people are particularly struggling with the Breaking of Bread service, and new converts also find it difficult. In Britain it is no different: where an assembly has a lively family service, the attendance will be much higher than at the Breaking of Bread: and young people often attend the Lord's Supper with some reluctance.

Our Breaking of Bread service is a product of 19th century English attitudes and is built around the culturally accepted qualities of that century. Solemnity, seriousness, silence, no music, no demonstrative action and a preference for meditation were all part of the lifestyle of the mid-19th century.

But the culture of today is totally different. We are in a time of action, involvement, musical expression, drama, bodily movement and feeling. It is no wonder that the world-wide renewal of worship that is going on today started in New Zealand among people who left the Brethren movement.

The 1st century Christians had to shake off the outmoded traditions of Judaism, and the early Brethren had to shake loose from the fixed forms of the church of England. Now, we must be big enough to keep our movement free from the deadening traditions of 19th century Brethrenism.

Frank Tillapaugh has said it over and over again: we are 'hilariously free' to adapt and change to help us get through to the culture of our day.

It is time to set people free to worship the Lord freely and fully. This means changing the whole pattern of our normal communion service to allow special music, poems, testimony, drama and other forms of worship that lift up Christ and honor and worship him.

We can set themes, plan worship around certain passages of Scripture, give leadership and direction, and bring back the freedom of the Spirit to a service we love and cherish.

Worship can become real and exciting, and the people will be caught up in a fresh vision of the risen Christ.

Why can't we have bands and musical instruments? Let's praise him with trumpets and guitars, and tambourines and strings, and flutes and cymbals as the Psalmist recommended.

Let's move away from the bondage of early British Brethren tradition and in our time worship the Lord in the beauty of holiness. There is nothing in the New Testament which prescribes our form of worship in the Breaking of Bread service.

We need to break into small groups and talk about the wonder of God. We need to clap and sing, making a joyful noise unto the Lord. We need to blend the traditional and the contemporary, allowing the Spirit of God free access among us.

A renewed, revitalized worship time will draw the Body together and set the stage for revival in our midst. Let's have the courage to bring about change at the Lord's supper. It will set a new, positive tone for the whole assembly.

2. Increased Emphasis on Prayer

It seems to me that there has been in the last ten years a massive deterioration in the emphasis on prayer in our midst. Very little prayer is being offered in our circles. I believe we need an all-out effort to get the church praying.

I believe the day of the typical mid-week prayer time is probably over. Our society militates against getting people out in mid-week to a prayer meeting. If we took a survey of those churches which still have a mid-week prayer meeting, both in Britain and America, we would probably find that only 10–25 percent of the believers attend.

Here are some alternative ideas:

1. Each Sunday provide a list of five things for the people to pray about that week.
2. Develop telephone prayer chains for special requests.
3. Form small home groups for personal growth and prayer.
4. Develop a quarterly evening of prayer; make it exciting, fast moving, specific.
5. Every three months have a prayer chain around the clock for 24 hours with people signing up for 15-minute segments.
6. Produce a card, 'Please be my prayer partner and pray with me for . . .'
   Make them available to the congregation or give them to people on an individual basis. Then ask other people in the congregation to take those cards and pray for the request for one week.

Only as we get back to a real emphasis on prayer will we see revival come. Prayer doesn't have to be in the forms of the past, but it *is* an essential ingredient and we must find contemporary ways to get people praying.

3. Leadership

I am firmly convinced that there is a difference between eldership and leadership. Eldership is an office; leadership is a gift. Not all elders are leaders.

In many churches the elders are all over 50 years in age and there is a desperate fear of adding anyone younger who doesn't come from a traditional Brethren background. We must break that cycle. Older men need to resign and let the 30 and 40 year olds take responsibility. If we are doing our job, they will be prepared by the Holy Spirit for the responsibility.

In addition, we must have leaders. We must find those with that gift, develop them, and set them free to lead. Some of us are trying to lead and are not succeeding. We need the grace to step aside and say, 'I am an elder or a full-time worker, but I am not a leader. I'll let someone else lead, and I'll support, encourage and help them in any way I can.'

Some are excellent Bible teachers, pastors, evangelists, but don't have the gift of leadership.

Who are the leaders in your church? Who has the gift of leadership or who can be developed? We urgently, desperately need to find them. Our ecclesiology has militated against allowing leadership to rise, and so our best people have gone to other churches and para-church ministries. We have refused to allow leadership to become evident and minister as God intended.

It is not a denial of the priesthood of all believers to have strong leadership. We have had a flaw in our thinking in this area. I know that our movement started as a reaction to clericalism in Britain, and we must continue to repudiate clericalism and individual authoritarianism.

But we have thrown the baby out with the bath water. We have denied one of the gifts God has given to his Church, and we need to change our ways. We need strong local leadership and we need national leadership that can guide and encourage our churches to growth and change.

Establishing solid leadership under the authority and guidance of the elders is a positive way to bring us back to a place where the Holy Spirit can start changing churches and renewing them by his power. Spirit-filled, wise leaders can be a catalyst to revival in our midst.

4. Recognition of Gifts

The leadership issue is a symptom of a deeper problem in our midst. That problem is the silence among us in helping people find, and use, their spiritual gifts.

I believe the elders or small group leaders should know the primary spiritual gifts of every member in the body. And we should be putting people to work in the body in the area of their giftedness.

We have passed by the teaching on gifts, and in almost every local church I know there are many people who don't know their gifts. In fact, people are recruited for and accept tasks within the church without any consideration of their gifts.

We need to have seminars where each person discovers their gifts . . . and then the elders need to provide ministries within the body where these gifts can be used for the glory of God. It will revolutionize the church, and it is another important step to revival.

Now, the last two areas of change relate to the community around us. I believe they are crucial if we are going to be impacting our society.

If a church has the right climate, and the power of the Holy Spirit at work, and is growing in worship, leadership, prayer and gift development, it is ready for an awakening that can bring a host of hurting people through the door.

The last two crucial areas are ones we must work on to accomplish this.

5. Preaching

The type of messages and style of community service is crucial today. We are in a far more sophisticated society than ever before in our history. Television, which is a major influencing factor, has changed the expectations of people.

People today want relevant subjects, upbeat, fast-moving programming that is constantly changing. Many short segments should make up the programme.

Fifteen minutes of singing and a 45-minute message won't attract the typical non-church goer today.

We need creative expressions such as:

* special musical numbers
* interviews
* congregational songs
* drama
* five-minute slide shows
* poems
* monologues
* a 25-minute message (maximum) . . .
. . . all packed into one hour!

The style of preaching is crucial to reach today's unchurched people. In our movement we must develop a whole new atmosphere about our Sunday morning community service if we intend to touch the hurting, broken people in our community.

On the street where I live there are 16 blocks of flats. There are yuppies, single people living together, lonely widows staying up to 2 or 3 am every night watching T.V. because they have no friends, turned off Catholics, liberal Protestants, alcoholics, and retired, bored people. If we are going to reach them, I want to bring them to a place where they will feel comfortable, and that means our preaching and programming style must change.

6. Evangelism

In the congregation probably only 10 per cent of the people have the gift of evangelism.

However, all of us have the responsibility of evangelism. If I attend a positive, vibrant morning service that I am confident in, then I will invite my neighbours. But when I have doubts and am not sure what is going to happen, or I am uneasy about the quality and consistency of the service, I will encourage them to go somewhere else where they'll really get the message in a form that doesn't turn them off.

My personal witness should tie into the church, for that is how churches grow. It is said that approximately 80 per cent of the new people attending church come because someone invited them. If I am not confident in the programme and atmosphere of the church, I am not going to bring my neighbours.

Now, finally, we must deal with how to make changes.

How to bring about change

First, I want to re-affirm to you that I am not talking about changing Scripture or in any way changing doctrine. I am talking about *methodology*. There are conservative and liberal churches regarding theology. We are the conservative variety. There are traditional and progressive churches regarding methodology. We must move from our present traditional stance to a progressive stance.

Second, I want to restate that change is not sacred in itself. Creativity for the sake of being clever is not valid.

Third, I must repeat that if you are in a place where there is little hope for change, then you mustn't beat your head against the wall for ten years and cause frustration and division. Leave.

Find another place where your life and ministry can be vitally used for God's glory and the expansion of his kingdom.

Larry Osborne suggests that there are four steps to take before you make a major change.

1. Test the Waters

Try to find out ahead of time how people will react should the change actually take place. Ask a cross-section of the people, elders, power brokers and average members what they think of an idea or possible change.

Ask their opinion, not in any official way, but quietly in small social settings. You are not looking for approval or disapproval, but just initial reactions.

This will give you valuable information on how to adjust the plan and you will know what aspects will cause the most resistance.

2. Listen and Respond to Resistors

Don't look at people as adversaries, but think of them as advisors. Take note of negative responses and work on clear, concise, specific answers. As you listen, you will find other people who have hidden agendas of what they want.

Maybe you can combine some of their desires and win those who might otherwise oppose you. Be very careful how you choose your words. Don't use inflammatory or strong words at inappropriate times. Often, if you change terminology, you can get the effect you want without significant resistance. While you should not give the resistors veto power, you must listen and this will help you often develop a better idea.

3. Convince Individuals Before Groups

Often we make the terrible mistake of taking the idea to the group of elders first. If you force people to make public their initial reactions, you are in for deep trouble. Often initial reactions to changes are negative, and usually public responses are permanent. When an elder opposes an idea in a meeting, it is very difficult for him to back down and change his position.

If you can sell enough individuals to give the idea credibility before it goes to the entire group, you will have much greater success. So, first get the 'main man' and make him the co-manager of the idea.

Second, go for the 10 per cent who will be most affected by the change.

Third, go for the key people—the people in the know—the core of the church, that is perhaps another 20 per cent. They need to be shared with and consulted so that the change isn't a surprise when it is announced.

Finally, let all the people know in plenty of time. Tell them it's coming, that it is getting closer, that it is here, and that it has been here, and that it is still here.

4. Lead Boldly

That doesn't mean running rough-shod over those who disagree, but it does mean not being hesitant or fearful. It means stepping out to make the change a success. Fear of upsetting a few can allow a handful of critics to hold off an army of supporters.

If you are convinced this is God's will, be bold. That means you have counted the cost. Often change means that you might lose a family or two, but if it results in five families replacing them and the programming becoming more attractive to the community, then you must weigh the cost and decide if you will go with it.

So, as you begin to think about change, let me summarize:

1. The power of the Holy Spirit is an absolute essential for spiritual life and growth in the church. Principles alone won't do the job.
2. Programmes won't work without the right spiritual climate. And that climate is made up of:
   * a positive atmosphere
   * a commitment to excellence
   * trust
   * flexibility
   * a servant spirit
3. The most urgent changes we must make are:
   * revitalizing the worship meeting
   * increasing the emphasis on prayer

   • leadership development
   • recognition of gifts
   • preaching
   • evangelism
4. To bring about the changes, you must:
   • test the waters
   • listen and respond to resistors
   • convince individuals before groups
   • lead boldly

I am committed to our movement. I have lived my life to encourage, support, change, renew and revitalize it. Sometimes I get discouraged. I wonder if it is really worth all the blood, sweat, tears, attacks, innuendos and criticisms that come my way.

But I tell you now that the Lord has done great things for me. He has rescued me from the pit of Hell. He has suffered abuse, criticism, defamation of character, spitting, scoffing, beating and crucifixion in order to redeem me.

And following Paul's example, I am willing to fill up the measure of the sufferings of Christ. So, if my ministry demands that I, too, suffer, I am willing to do it.

I want to be in the arena where the action is, and I'll fight, and work, and preach, and dream, and act till God calls me home. This is a day for soldiers. The battle is raging. You can count the cost and join the forces.

And if we go forward in the power of God, I am confident that in our generation we will see a new, vibrant group of churches accepting the challenge, and experiencing not only the agony of change but also the ecstasy of revival.

And I intend to be a part of them.

Questions for Discussion

Biblical

1. This chapter says that we need 'a framework which is comprised of a few basic principles that don't change'. It then suggests four of those basic principles. Do you agree with the

list? From your biblical understanding of the nature of the church, are there some you would query, or others you would add?

2. 'Let's move away from the bondage of early British Brethren tradition . . . There is nothing in the New Testament which prescribes our form of worship in the Breaking of Bread service.' Do you agree?

3. Four steps are listed which should be taken before a church makes a major change. Do you agree with them? Can you find biblical examples (e.g. Moses? Nehemiah?) of people who applied these principles in bringing change?

Practical

1. 'If you are doing the same thing you were doing ten years ago, or even five years ago, something is wrong.' Do you agree?

2. Why do you think it is that churches are more resistant to change than most other social institutions?

3. 'If you are in a place where there is little hope for change, then don't beat your head against the wall for ten years and cause frustration and division. Leave.' Is this the most realistic thing to do?

Action

1. This chapter suggests 'five measurements you can take to see if you have the right climate'. How does your church measure up to these criteria? Where are you weakest?

2. Kevin Dyer also suggests 'six urgent changes that need to be made in most churches'. Do they apply to yours? If so, which are most pressing?

3. Are your leaders good at introducing change? Have they anything to learn from the section headed 'How to bring about change'?

Chapter 4

Vision

A cartoon was passed around our office a couple of years ago. In it were two Eskimos sitting on chairs, fishing through holes in the ice. The one on the right was sitting with his line in a hole about the size of a small manhole. The Eskimo on the left was also sitting with his line in the water. His hole, however, reached almost to the end of the lake. It was about the size and shape of a whale.

Now that is vision. He is thinking big. The time he spent getting ready to fish was enormous. He wore out several saws cutting the ice. But he is ready for anything. He's expecting a big fish. This Eskimo has vision.

How do you think the other Eskimo felt sitting next to this guy with the huge hole? My guess is that every now and again he looked over and wondered if he should cut his hole bigger. You see, vision is contagious, and even though it sometimes looks foolish, it can have a profound affect on others.

Chuck Swindoll tells the story of a couple of nuns who worked as nurses in a hospital. They ran out of petrol while driving to work one morning. A service station was nearby, but they had no containers in which to put the needed petrol.

One of the women remembered they had a bedpan in the trunk of the car, so the fuel was poured into the bedpan and they carried it carefully back to the car.

As the nuns were pouring the gasoline from the bedpan into the fuel tank, two men drove by and stared in disbelief. Finally one said to the other, 'Now, Fred, that's what I call faith.'

It appeared to be foolish. The trouble was those doubters just didn't have the facts. And were they ever surprised when those nuns went ripping past them on the motorway.

So much of what we undertake lacks vision. We cut our tiny holes in the ice and make plans to go home cold and hungry.

Vision is the blazing campfire around which the people of God should gather. It provides light, energy, warmth and unity, but many of us stand away in the shadows and refuse to come up to the fire and be a part of the vision.

In 1886, the U.S. patent office was very nearly closed because some congressmen didn't want to include it in the budget. One congressman said, 'It now appears that everything practical has already been invented.' That was before telephones, computers, cars, airplanes, and a million other inventions.

'Without a vision the people perish,' warns the writer of Proverbs. That word perish can be translated 'run wild' or 'get out of hand'. Unless people are challenged by visionaries, it is so easy for the people of God to move on to something or somewhere else. They run wild, or get out of hand instead of having definitive goals and plans to accomplish something really significant.

One of the major reasons our movement continues to lose people is that we lack vision. There is nothing that excites people and motivates people like a vision to accomplish something special.

Who has a vision in your church and how is it communicated to the people? Helen Keller, that wonderful blind, deaf and speechless woman, said, 'The greatest tragedy to befall a person is to have sight but lack vision.'

That's true of churches too. As a body of believers, we have sight. Our eyes have been opened to the glory of the risen Christ, but all too often we lack vision.

The Bible is full of visionaries. The 11th chapter of Hebrews lists some for us. By faith, Noah built a boat before God invented rain. By faith, Abraham led the first tour of the Holy Land without a round trip ticket.

By faith, Moses led two million Israelites into the wilderness where there wasn't a grocery store or a delicatessen for hundreds of miles.

These are called high-risk ventures, and the Bible is full of them. Paul says in Romans 15:20, 'It has always been my ambition to preach the Gospel where Christ was not known.' He was a visionary. He didn't want to go where everyone else had been. He didn't want to do what everyone else did. He had a vision for the unreached areas of the world.

In the last few centuries Hudson Taylor, George Müller, C.T. Studd, William Tyndale, Martin Luther, William Booth and long lines of others have been high risk venturers.

But where have all the high risk venturers gone? There are still a few around today—colourful evangelicals with a vision to make a difference in the world and in the Church. But God is looking for more visionaries. In our movement we are desperately weak in encouraging and helping the 'old men to dream dreams and the young men to see visions'.

1. Vision Defined

Vision is a comprehensive sense of where you are, where you are going, how you are going to get there, and what you will do after you get there. It is dreaming dreams about the future. It is seeing the big picture and personally painting a part of it.

Vision is feeling challenged by the world around and being compelled to make a mark on it through the force of our own ideas, personality, resources and desires.

Now vision must be focused. If it is too broad people will flounder and become discouraged. If it is non-specific it is useless. It must be clear, concise and in focus. Blurry vision causes people to lose their way.

The vision must also be reachable. On the one hand we must not limit vision, but on the other hand a comprehensive vision is often too much for a small congregation. It is essential that we recognize our limits, narrow the focus, define the priorities and gear expectations accordingly.

A church must have manageable goals and strategy to reach them, otherwise it can become overwhelmed and paralyzed. With a clear vision and measurable goals that are attainable, we are more likely to experience the joy and impetus of success.

Defining vision is often very difficult. Each local body is a unique expression with different gifts, callings and ministries. Some emphasize missions, others worship or small group fellowships. Still others major on evangelism or teaching.

Most churches don't like to admit they specialize. We all want to be full service churches even when we don't have the resources to do it. The result is that we are often bland and mediocre. To accomplish one vision well, we may have to sacrifice something else.

Even though we may be weak in some areas, it is better to have a vision and develop our strengths until we have the resources to develop other areas of interest. Churches must focus their efforts. We can always enlarge our boundaries later, but it is vital that we set priorities, determine the best use of our resources and pace ourselves.

So as we face the issue of vision, we need to see into the distance where we want to be five years from now, and tackle the ministry one project at a time.

It will take stretching and straining, but when there is a consensus of the long range vision, and we have found a reasonable starting point, we can move forward step by step to reach the vision we have set. Unfortunately, many churches have lost their vision, or they have no vision at all. We are content to be what we've always been without any vision for the future.

Dag Hammarskjöld, the former Secretary General of the United Nations, relates the story of a man who sailed with Columbus when he discovered America. In his diary he wrote, 'I hope I get back home and get the job at the cobbler's shop down the road from where I live.' Hammarskjöld's perceptive insight was this: Here was a man on a journey discovering new worlds, yet he could not see beyond his street.

Lift up your eyes—look ahead—catch a vision. God can and will do great things if we have a clear sense of the Holy Spirit's direction and we step out on the promises of God.

2. Vision Developed

As a vision is developed, there are two key questions to be answered.

First, do the people own the vision?

The key to making vision useful is for its possessor to share it with those who do not possess it but who can support it. The people need to understand the vision and begin to see it as their own. They may not have originally had the vision, but they should grow to understand it, support it and ultimately own it.

If a vision is a one-man show, ram-rodded through the elders and on to the people, it will soon die. There must be time taken to 'sell' the vision to others. Most people don't automatically accept a new vision. Usually there is resistance. The time spent developing vision and communicating it is well worth all the effort.

The second key question to be answered is—Do we have the resources?

We must clearly evaluate what resources are available and develop vision within the context of those resources, or be very sure that the Lord is going to provide the resources from the outside.

Proverbs 18:13 says, 'What a shame, yes how stupid, to decide not knowing the facts.' A shortage of resources doesn't close the door on the vision but it means we must weigh the personnel demands and costs and find out if we are prepared to pay to make the vision real.

Sometimes it is necessary to stretch painfully to achieve the vision, but what rewards there are once the vision is fulfilled. At other times we must simply take a step of implicit faith, knowing clearly that God is leading us forward.

If God has given us the vision and the ability to anticipate the resources, then we should give an automatic 'yes' to the vision. However, if either of these ingredients (the people owning the vision and the available resources) is missing or uncertain, then perhaps we should say, 'Not yet.'

Now if the people own the vision and the resources are available, then we must find the leadership people to make the vision a reality.

In this regard I remember clearly some mistakes I have made at International Teams. Several years ago I had a wonderful vision. I thought, 'Wouldn't it be great if we could have a shortwave radio system so that we could regularly talk to our teams overseas.' I thought it would save us a lot of money and heartache if we could simply call them on a weekly basis and talk back and forth for a half hour. It could really enable us to keep up to date with current events in a way we never could before.

Well, I talked a staff member into going to school and getting his licence to operate a shortwave radio. We got the equipment and put up a big antenna. But you know, the staff member's heart wasn't in it and he was too busy with all the other more important things to do. So everything sat in boxes for about seven years and finally a few months ago we sold the whole thing.

I've learned that promoting ideas and programmes isn't the way to do it. You've got to promote qualified people with the vision. I had all the equipment, but I didn't have an operator with the vision. You can have a printing press, but unless you have a printer with a vision for a ministry in printing, all the good equipment in the world won't get the job done.

My best ideas or plans are void of life until they are shouldered by a person with a genuine vision of how God could use it to further his kingdom. My goal now is to support people with a vision, not simply programmes.

If the vision dies, we should let the programme die a quiet death as well. Otherwise, some well-meaning person will be exhausted trying to maintain something for which he or she has no heart.

Lawrence Stanhope is 84 years of age and he took out a patent on a space garden. It will be a one-acre plot that is planted on a platform (about eight miles above the earth) that zooms west at exactly the same speed the earth rotates east. It will experience perpetual sunshine so he has multi-tiers that take turns moving to the top. It will be flying at about 1200 miles an hour, 24 hours a day. Lawrence Stanhope has a vision. He can see continuously growing gardens in space. Remember, he is 84.

Some of us, much younger, rarely dream or think creatively. We go on with the same routine year after year. Stop and grab yourself by the back of the neck and ask: what new idea have you tried lately to advance the cause of Christ? What dream keeps you awake at night? What fresh idea will revolutionize your church or ministry? How can you develop this vision so others will get excited about joining you in changing your world?

People of vision are not afraid to fail. There will always be problems and discouragers who can't see beyond the first obstacle. I'm glad Edison didn't give up on the light bulb even though his helpers seriously doubted the thing would ever work.

I'm glad Lindberg decided to ignore what everyone else said was ridiculous and was flirting with death.

I'm glad Luther refused to back down when the church doubled her fists and clenched her teeth. I'm glad Papa Ten Boom said 'yes' to frightened Jews who needed a safe haven and hiding place. I'm glad Wilberforce persisted for forty years in fighting slavery throughout the British dominions.

I'm glad that our Lord Jesus left heaven and went all the way to the cross for the vision of bringing many sons and daughters to glory.

Don't be afraid to go forward even though there are many problems. God is looking for men and women of vision. People with wholehearted commitment to making a difference in our world.

Develop creativity, develop practicality, develop perseverance and be driven to succeed. With God as your guide and the Holy Spirit as your power, you can move forward with vision and vitality to see the work of God advance.

3. Vision Directed

The conception of vision, the gestation of plans and the carrying to delivery must all be pursued in an unabashed spirit of prayer and dependency upon the Holy Spirit. There is no question about the fact that we need Holy Spirit unction in the direction and dreams of ministry.

But it is equally true that we must have people willing to put their hands and minds to work to make the vision happen. I believe the person willing to shoulder the responsibility for a part of the vision must also have the privilege of making most of the key decisions about that part of the vision.

There is a clear equation that needs to be followed—

RESPONSIBILITY + TIME + ENERGY = PRIVILEGE

Our problem today is that whenever vision rears its head in our midst, it is whittled away by people who have the privilege of decision making without the commitment of time, energy and responsibility.

Everyone wants to have their say in the direction of the

ministry, but very few are willing to put their time and energy into making it happen. There is no greater killer of vision than person with power making decisions without being an activator and participant in the vision.

I believe the elders or deacons, depending on the issue, should decide whether to give the go ahead to the person with the vision. If the answer is 'yes' then that person should be set free to live and work to make the vision happen.

All too often we restrict, confine, reduce and delete. We take the spirit out of visionaries. That's why they go off and start para-church organizations where they are free from bureaucratic denuding of vision.

It is people who have vision. Programmes don't have vision. People must be allowed greater opportunities to do their thing for God's work. We must constantly look for new gifts in the church and allow them to enlarge the vision within the area of their giftedness.

There is a local assembly that I know well that was coasting downhill on a one-hundred-year history. The glory of the past was long overshadowed by a group of kind, godly elders who were strictly maintainers and had no vision for the future.

Three men, one about 50 years of age, another about 40, and the other about 30, went to the elders and laid out a plan of action. It was made very clear that unless change took place, the church would lose quite a few of the young families they had.

The elders admitted that things weren't going well. So they set the three men free to make changes and to develop a vision for the assembly. The 50-year-old man took the leadership of the vision, the other two committed to backing him up with time, energy and responsibility.

The three men took a survey in the church and found out that people felt comfortable with friendship evangelism. Many of the people weren't able to do aggressive personal evangelism, but most felt they could meet people easily and be friendly.

So they decided to make the church known in the community as the friendliest church in town. They changed the morning service to meet the needs of the unchurched and they went on a high profile programme to 'sell' the assembly as a place where people would be accepted and loved.

People began to hear about this place, and before long some young counter-culture people began to come. It was pretty hard for some of the older believers, but most of them swallowed their pride and prejudices and accepted these non-traditional young people.

From then on the work started to grow so that today the assembly is well over twice, and moving toward three times the size of the original group. A decision was made to free the assembly for a vision that some of the young men had.

Many have been saved, and added to the church, and the growth of that traditional, staid assembly has been unbelievable. It *can* be done. But vision must be managed by clear, consistent leadership.

Paul says in 1 Corinthians 14:8, 'If the trumpet does not sound a clear call, who will get ready for battle?' Confusion on leadership of the vision will result in diminished accomplishments. There must be a clear, concise sound ringing out throughout the church. This is the vision. Here is the leader. This is the way we are going.

Strong leadership of a vision coupled with prayer and faith is an almost unbeatable combination. Weak leadership with an indistinct sound spells doom for vision.

4. Vision Dreams

Visionaries are never happy accomplishing goals. In my own experience I find I automatically push the goal further out as soon as I begin to get close to accomplishing it. Or if it is fully accomplished, I set a new goal before I finally wind up the last one.

It is only this kind of dreaming and this kind of discipline that saves you from coasting and being contented. We need a holy discontent with things as they are. It doesn't matter how good it seems, it can still be improved.

A fresh, creative look at something that is going well will often allow us to make it go with excellence.

As we dream about the future, we must resist the pressure to be a supermarket church stocking everything imaginable. We can be content to start out being a specialty shop. Do a few things with excellence first before branching out.

We sometimes sing, 'Jesus doeth all things well', but *we* may have to be content with doing one or two things well to begin with. We should stick with those few things until such a time as we are ready to add new areas to the vision. One or two victories will encourage the body to go on to greater steps of faith.

Before Columbus discovered the 'new world', Portugal's flag had a Latin phrase on it, *'Ne plus ultra'*, referring to Portugal's position at the western end of Europe, jutting out into the Atlantic Ocean. This motto meant 'nothing more beyond'. After 1492 and the discovery of the new world, the slogan was changed to *'Plus ultra'* (more beyond).

People of vision can change the whole atmosphere in an assembly by looking to the horizon and seeing more beyond. We don't have to settle for the status quo. We don't have to give way to mediocrity. We don't have to accept substandard programmes. We don't have to be bound in tradition and mired in bureaucracy. We can change things, but we have to be men and women of vision.

Vision starts out very much as an attitude. What we see depends mainly on what we look for. And if we are looking for a spiritual awakening, then we are going to have to be activists in the areas of vision and change.

5. Vision Dangers

Along the vision road there are many dangers. These are potholes we can fall into which will impede our journey.

The first danger is the 'Big is beautiful and blessed' syndrome.

A lot of people fall into this pothole. They get a vision and they come to believe that because they are expanding and have a big vision that it automatically receives the blessing of God.

Bigness is not wrong or right. The bigger the better philosophy isn't true. Bigness is not a sign of the blessing of God. However, neither is smallness a sign of God's approval. The faithful few who are standing for God and going nowhere is not an evidence of the Spirit's work.

Communism is big; so are Coca Cola, the Egyptian pyramids, the state of Texas and elephants. Should we assume the Holy Spirit prospered them all?

On the other hand, the Ku Klux Klan is small; so are cancer cells, bullets and a vial of poison.

Neither bigness nor smallness have anything to do with vision. Large churches need vision and small churches need vision. Large churches must grow and small churches must grow. And if they don't, the candlestick of testimony can easily flicker out.

The second danger is the 'What's good for business' philosophy.

There are enormous pressures today to baptize technology, organization and secular philosophies so they can be sanctified for use in the church. Just because it is good for business doesn't automatically mean it is good for the church.

Now I am the first one to say I want to use everything I can to expand the kingdom of God. I believe we should have sharp, contemporary ministries that attract people. And I want to use organization and technology to accomplish that end. But if we depend on it to do the Lord's work, we have missed the whole impact of the necessity of the Holy Spirit's power flowing through people who use these things for the glory of God.

The third danger is the 'Miracles by methods' approach.

Closely aligned with the 'what's good for business' philosophy is this idea that we can produce miracles by good methodology.

Techniques are not wrong in themselves, but we must not rely on them to raise money or get a crowd. It is easy to get good results and then claim that God is blessing our faith, when actually all that is happening is that we have pulled all the right strings.

It is miracles by the Holy Spirit's intervention that we need. If all that we have is miracles by human methods, then we have been guilty of spiritual abortion. We have thwarted the purposes of God and acted in the flesh.

The fourth danger is the 'Daredevil' philosophy.

Some people allow their vision to get them way out on a limb for God and then they expect other people to rescue them. If we are filled with unrealistic dreams and schemes using other people's money, we are in great danger.

When the person with the vision has little personal risk in the vision, then beware. Visionaries must be prepared to lay their lives on the line too. It needs to cost the visionary something to live the vision.

A daredevil philosophy of making a big plan and expecting everyone else to pay for it without too much cost personally is a dangerous position to play.

The fifth danger is the 'Empire-builder syndrome'.

Many Christian leaders need to examine their motivation to see if they are building for themselves or for the Lord. It is very easy to get a complex as being the saviour or the leader of the assembly. We must guard against this subtle form of sin at all costs. We must build effective ministries *for the Lord*. Building personal empires will result in poverty of spirit and powerless living.

The sixth danger is to compromise the truth for the sake of the vision.

We must never forsake the truth of Scripture to accomplish a good end. We must never distort the truth of Scripture to gain a following.

Unfortunately today we have popularized Christianity to such an extent that we find that we can be good Christians in our society and still be guilty of worldly living.

The seventh danger is to buy into the philosophy that 'shoddiness is godliness.'

There is little that saddens me more than to go to a place where Christian ministry is being carried out and find it to be in a state of disrepair. Excellence is not extravagance. We need to demand excellence in all we do.

We should be sending our personnel to seminars constantly to upgrade their skills. We should be giving regular appraisals of our fulltime workers and missionaries. We should demand accountability and not be slip-shod in our approach to the Lord's work.

'Decently and in order' means exactly that. Sloppy planning, foolish management and overspending should not be found among us. It is time to demand of our para-church organizations and our local churches a sense of accountability and responsibility.

How is it that we are lackadaisical in these areas? It is because we have bought into the philosophy that people are accountable only to the Lord; and the Bible doesn't teach that at all.

Only God's records will reveal who are the men and women with real vision in this generation, but I think we all should strive to renew our desire to push forward the work of the Lord in our time.

As a group of men and women, let us be committed to renewing vision in our movement. We must get off our seats and dream and plan creatively. We need to cry out to the Holy Spirit to revitalize us. We must move forward to mobilize people to join us on a march that would send us out to be radical followers of Jesus Christ in a world that desperately needs him.

This is the vision—let us join hands to do it in our day.

Questions for Discussion

Biblical

1. 'Vision' is not a word the Bible uses very much. (And when it does, it is usually talking about supernatural visitations, not the kind of 'visionary thinking' which Kevin Dyer is describing here.) So is he correct to attach so much importance to having vision?

2. Some Christians would say, 'It is required that we are *faithful*, not successful (1 Cor 4:2, Matt 25:21). This book is trying to turn us all into activists, and we're not all cut out for it!' Is that a fair criticism?

3. 'Churches must focus their efforts . . . it is vital that we set priorities, determine the best use of our resources and pace ourselves.' Can you see any evidence of this kind of strategy in the way Paul went about his missionary work?

Practical

1. How can a church decide what its vision ought to be? How

should it work out its goals and a strategy for reaching them? And how should it ensure that everyone 'owns' the vision?

2. 'We go on with the same routine year after year.' Why are churches so prone to do this? How can we ensure a flow of new ideas, a constant renewing of the vision, a regular re-evaluation of what we spend our time on?

3. How can we tell when we are pushing forward too ambitiously? How can we tell when we are holding back with unnecessary caution?

Action

1. 'If the vision dies, we should let the programme die a quiet death as well.' Are there activities in your church programme for which nobody has much of a vision any more? If there were, how would you know and what would you do about it?

2. Seven 'vision dangers' are listed in the chapter. Do any of them threaten your work? Could they?

3. 'There is no greater killer of vision than people with power making decisions without being an activator and participant in the vision.' Is that a danger in your situation? Are there changes you should make to avoid it?

4. Finally—how has reading this book changed your vision for your church? What must you now do as a result of reading it?

The Rat-i Maggot

and Other Poems

Roundhead Publications

ISBN: 09532812 05

Published by Roundhead Publications
PO Box 668, Portslade, E Sussex BN42 4BG.
Tel: 01273 870875   Fax: 01273 870866

Typesetting by Martin Cooper (with thanks to Brunswick Marketing)
Printed in Great Britain by Antony Rowe Ltd, Chippenham, Wiltshire.
Front cover and lugworm illustration by Nick Staples
All other illustrations by Womble
Back cover photo by Gair Dunlop

For Joy

Acknowledgements

The poems in this, my third collection, have been performed in rock venues, arts centres, theatres, pubs, universities, cafes, schools, libraries, open air festivals, autonomous anti-fascist youth centres, squats and God knows where else in the UK, Australia, Canada, New Zealand, Ireland, the US, Germany, Holland, Scandinavia, Romania, Bulgaria, Austria and the Basque Country.

Some have wormed their way on to international, national and local radio and TV and into the Guardian newspaper; many more are to be found in innumerable fanzines and small publications; two are included in 'Build a Bonfire', the stirring story of our battle to save Brighton & Hove Albion Football Club (Mainstream Publications); 'Sarajevo' and 'The Blandford Forum' are song lyrics brought to life by my band Barnstormer on our debut album 'The Siege of Shoreham.'

Thanks to all those comrades and fellow-travellers who ignite and inspire me through the hogsheads and corkscrews of my poetic path – you know who you are – and to Messrs Hilaire Belloc and Joseph Porter for some welcome yardsticks.

For this book: total homage is due to Barnstormer guitarist and Fish Brother Martin Cooper for typesetting, to Womble and Nick Staples for the illustrations and to Joy Scully for her invaluable editorial guidance.

Attila, February 1998

Contents

SONGS

with illustrations
by Womble

The British Bullfrog

Six-inch sperm in garden centre
Strange, zygotic waggle dance
Disembodied, black placenta
Hitched a ride with foreign plants.
Uninvited and unwanted.
Poet says 'I'll take them home'
Four enormous bullfrog tadpoles
in my pond and free to roam.

Press release from the Home Office:
It's a witchhunt, there's no doubt.
'Catch these immigrant amphibians!
They're illegal – stamp them out!
They'll wipe out our native species . . .'
(Don't tell me: they're weird, they smell,
nick our jobs and shag our pond life
and they're on the dole as well.)

Crashing down, the eco-jackboot . . .
'No, they can't stay in your pond!
You'll be fined at least a thousand
If you let these things abscond!'
Semen-like, they squirm in protest.
'Freedom for the Southwick 4!'
But I know the awful verdict:
Custody for evermore.

One year in an old aquarium
then this macro-spunk grows legs
Diet of red meat and chicken –
turn their snouts up at ants' eggs . . .

One year more and they are sorted
Saved from eco-nazi doom
Summer: big pit in the garden.
Winter: in my living room.

Now their diet is worms and crickets
(Big worms and big crickets, sure.)
Grow two inches every year
Soon a foot long – even more!
They'll be hunting bigger victims
and the poet has a plan
Vengeance on the great oppressor
from my huge pitbullfrog clan . . .

Cats kill frogs – I've seen them do it
As a kid that lesson learned
Saw the corpse and shook with anger –
soon the tables will be turned.
Pampered Kitty meets the posse
Bullfrogs think 'Mmm . . . nice and fat:
one rich owner: what's the flavour?
Yes! Our favourite! Kit-e-Kat!'

Feline diet makes them bigger
Hungrier and sharper still
Militant amphibian army
Huge of mouth and iron of will.
Tories, fascists, High Court judges
Down their throats the same old way
as they croak 'No deportations!
British Bullfrogs – here to stay!'

The Maggot

The Maggot's not for recipes, at least that's my advice.
It's true that he looks rather like a wriggly grain of Rice
But don't use him in Puddings, don't serve him up with Curry
'cos if you do your Dinner Guests will leave in quite a hurry . . .
He's best for catching Barbel, Dace, Perch, Gudgeon, Bream and Bleak
(To make him wriggle when it's cold, just warm him in your Cheek.)
His Pupa's called a Caster, and is used for Castor Oil*
that's why it tastes revolting and makes Small Children recoil . . .
And, after several days as Caster, turns into a Fly
(an Insect you'll find on Neglected Pets after they Die)
So if you don't like the Maggot, I have only this to say:
Just make sure that the Children feed the Hamster every day . . .

this may actually not be true

3

The Rat-tailed Maggot

I'm sure the Maggot makes you feel quite ill.
The Rat-tailed Maggot's more unsettling still!
You'll find him in a stagnant, foetid Pool
(a Cattle-trough's a good place as a rule)
Suspended upside down, his usual station
Feasting on Decomposing Vegetation
and breathing through a Membranous Extension
which penetrates the water's surface tension.
When grown, our dear Protagonist pupates
(along with many thousands of his mates)
in dried-up hollows made from Cattle Piss.
And then – the final metamorphosis –
Insect so foul . . . Alack! What's this I see?
A Drone Fly. Pretty. Like a stingless bee.
(Thwarted, the Poet flies into a rage . . .)
But oh, what Glory in the Larval Stage!

The Crayfish

I had a large blue Crayfish.
The Scots would call him 'bonnie.'
His tank was in my living room.
I called my Crayfish Ronnie.

He had a spouse. Called Reggie.
He'd oft inseminate her.
Then one day something went amiss
and nasty Ronnie ate her.

And that's not all there was to it –
he ate his children too.
I phoned a Crayfish expert.
He said 'Crayfish often do.'

So Ronnie, brutal murderer
was put in solitary
with plastic plants and nothing else
to keep him company.

The coward got his just deserts:
I bought the Axolotl.
As Axl prowled, so Ronnie cowered:
Yes, Ronnie lost his botl!

The Lugworm

If Male and, shall we say, Under-Endowed
and shrivelled yet still further by the Sea
The Lugworm is a Beast to make you proud.
So dig one up: examine carefully
his Manly Shape, a full three inches long.
Thin at the bottom, thicker in the Gland.
A vulnerable Bell, and then a Hole.
He hangs, all wet and floppy, in your hand.
And now, perchance, think on the Angler's Hook
which penetrates the Creature at the Tip . . .
'Enough!' you cry. You're right! I'll stop right there
As howls of protest rise beneath my Zip . . .

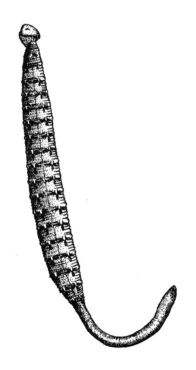

The Slug

Mollusc for sure, but Aperitif? Non-starter.
Not the cachet of the Oyster, I regret . . .
In truth, my friend, you have few Redeeming Features
And even I do not want you as a Pet.
Time after time my Lover's soft face will harden
as I approach with you nestling in my Palm
When she insists that you're thrown in Next Door's Garden
I will comply, although I wish you no harm.
Poor, homeless Snail. Pray, do you sell the Big Issue?
Ugly for sure, but you have efficient Glands . . .
Few Football Chairmen are actually this slimy –
Over the fence now! Time to wash my hands!

The Axolotl

The Axolotl is a beast unsung.
  It stays a Larva. It's forever young.
    If Nature ran its course, the Axolotl
      would be a Salamander. But it's notl.

The Lemming

The Lemming is the Ultimate Commuter –
same set-faced stare, same grey determination.
When Instinct says his final day has come
he sets off grimly for his Destination.
'Be quick!' says Mrs. Lemming, unaware
'I'm cooking you your favourite meal tonight . . .'
The booking clerk asks 'Single or return?
Oh, sorry, single. You're a Lemming, right?
But hang on, sir – they've got an offer on.
It's cheaper if you get a day return
And my mate's mum's in the Samaritans . . .'
Such laudable, compassionate concern!
But we, who clone our Sheep and Vegetables
without so much as a remorse-filled Sniff
Will ne'er hold back that unseen, mighty Hand
that sends a Lemming to his final Cliff . . .

The Don't Care Bear

The Don't Care Bear's got purple hair
A padlock round his neck
His dad says 'That's no son of mine!'
His mum's a nervous wreck . . .
He lives on Chips and Special Brew –
not soppy stuff like Honey
You'll find him in the underpass
(He'll ask you for some money)
He's got a mate called Tigger
and another one called Owl
They're in a band called 'PUNK'S NOT DEAD!'
They make the neighbours howl . . .
His parents named him Jeremy
His mates all call him Pooh
Says 'A.A. Milne's a wanker!
D'you want some Special Brew?'

Alan Sugar, Spurs chairman, was part of the Football Association team
which did the deal giving Rupert Murdoch's Sky TV exclusive rights to
broadcast Premiership football matches. Sugar is chairman of Amstrad,
one of the country's leading manufacturers of satellite dishes.
As for Murdoch – well, he wants the world . . .

A Sugared Dish

High in the sky the angler sits
in smug anticipation
No boundaries now hold back his dream
of global domination
Across the world his lines are cast
and now he lies in wait:
he's fishing for the human mind
and football is the bait.

The Premiership's a sugared dish
so swiftly, cleverly bought
It's good bait, but he needs some more:
he buys up every sport
The fish bite: he removes their guts
and leaves one single eye
fixed on the Sun and CNN:
One folk, one state, one Sky.

The rich elite rake in the cash –
it only flows one way
the small clubs teeter on the brink
some pinstriped vulture's prey
Developers eye up the grounds
whole lives are built upon
while Southerners in Man U shirts
switch televisions on.

The angler plays monopoly –
the government connives.
The shoals of fish swarm round the dish
which brightens up their lives
And Murdoch nears his killer goal:
a global superstate
where minds are caught and minds are set
and football is the bait.

Comic in a Basket

For a culture which sold its birthright: for the few, especially Mark Thomas, who remain as angry and dangerous as ever: and in hope that an emerging new breed will blast the game show fodder into history.

This is the tale of my times
the place where I started from
The friends and contemporaries
I've now parted from
A story of belief
of pride
of how it has to be
for Attila MC
It's all about perspectives
compromise
choices
paths going different ways
different voices
those who gave up
and those who still attack
and wanna talk back
It's all about England in these dull old days
where everyone obeys
and hacks say it's 'old hat'
to shout the odds and seethe
and say what you believe
It's the battle of ideas
It's the fight for proper beers
and it'll go on for years
and years and years
I stand for my words and for decent beer too
If you advertise chemical piss

this rap's especially for you
I'd rather sniff glue

Talking cutting edge gone blunt, blunt, blunt
Talking saboteurs now riding with the hunt
Talking cutting edge gone blunt, blunt, blunt
Talking saboteurs now riding with the hunt

Right in your face
and I'm not gonna mask it
MC Attila on the case
of the comic in a basket

*　　　*　　　*　　　*

I've earned my living as a poet since 1982
Didn't know it was that long?
Now you do
In fact I started a couple of years before
Blagged spots at punk gigs –
they wanted more
Peel sessions, albums, gigs in the rock scene
going to places most poets had never been
And then a whole new scene began
it was a good plan
sure, from time to time it could get a bit tame
but it was a fine game
London circuit
they called it New Variety
some kind of underground cultural society
a new breed got the chance to spread the word
and get our voices heard

For three or four years we all stood together
poets, comedians, musicians, whatever
as long as you were sharp and had something to say
the people were with you
it was OK
but defeat on defeat on defeat on defeat
put the whole of our culture on the retreat
and a radical attack was no longer hip –
all the rats left the sinking ship.

Comic in a basket.

New Variety became 'alternative comedy'
– losing all its cultural diversity
Alternative comedy became 'new comedy'
– losing its political suss and energy
New comedy became simply 'comedy'
– corporate mainstream TV commodity
'Got a new ad for Aims of Industry?
I'm a comedian: give it to me!'

Now comedy's so dull
and safe
and bland
it's time to make a stand
No bite
no attitude
it's not even funny
– and it's all about money.
Gag every ten seconds or you're history
Scriptwriting gag team: comedy factory
Roll on, roll off – are you with the agency?
'Too controversial: no good for TV!'

Comedy to go, careers in comedy
– comic in a basket
Comedy package, corporate hospitality
– comic in a basket
Seventies TV, old people, shopping
– routine routine
Seventies TV, old people, shopping
– routine routine

'Very funny' (Daily Express)
– comic in a basket
'Hilarious' (Daily Mail)
– comic in a basket
Get your dicks out for the banks
and give your sponsors grateful thanks.
Edinburgh Fringe?
Comedy trade fair.
Miss it if you dare!
Movers and shakers.
Radio and TV.
Me! Me! Me! Me!

Talking cutting edge gone blunt, blunt, blunt
Talking saboteurs now riding with the hunt
Talking cutting edge gone blunt, blunt, blunt
Talking saboteurs now riding with the hunt

Punter in a basket comedy club –
braying student Sun reader fun pub –
'Tell us a joke or we'll get rough
and lay off that political poetry stuff!'

But politics is people's lives
not fashion
and I burn with passion
My culture and beliefs run very deep
and I'm no sheep
So one fine day I handed in my cards
didn't find it hard.
Bollocks to comedy – I've got my own scene
Radical poet, Sydney to Aberdeen
Life is humour
music
politics
rage
I want them all on stage
But I keep in touch with my old friends
and I'm hip to the trends
I watch the scene from time to time and curse:
It's getting worse!
The Browbeaten Broadcasting Corporation
cowed by years of intimidation
is putting out pap that's reached a brand new low
Bass –
how low can you go?
Throwaway garbage game show lobotomese
Mad Cower Disease!
'Wanna be the star of Tacky Tabloid Tease?'
'Ooh ooh yes please!'
Comic in a basket's radio TV game show
about game shows in history.

'What's that advert from '73?'
'Who was in that situation comedy?'
Crap TV
about crap TV.
Radio in need of radiotherapy.
Recycled sheep in a bovine society.
Audiovisual BSE.

Gland in hand in the land of the bland, no stand
– comic in a basket
'Keep to the script as planned or you'll get banned!'
– comic in a basket
Some of you were mates, I don't like to offend ya
but I'm rapping for a brand new agenda

Talking cutting edge gone blunt, blunt, blunt
talking saboteurs now riding with the hunt
Talking cutting edge gone blunt, blunt, blunt
talking saboteurs
now riding
with
the
hunt!

The Mandelson Violin Concerto

I'm the conductor
That means I'm in charge.
I know you loathe me.
Don't B sharp
or you'll end up flat.
Yes, I know the other lot
played that piece solidly
for eighteen years
but Terry Wogan likes it
so we've made it our theme tune.
It's not why you joined the orchestra?
You've been here 30 years?
Tough.
Yes, I know it's supermarket muzak
– all majors, no miners –
but it certainly strikes a chord.
Did you read that great review in the Daily Mail?
Play along,
smile, sweetly,
or you're out of the orchestra.
. If you want the Red Flag
join the SWP.
We're the Mike Flowers Pops.

Designated Areas

I know this doesn't sound very poetic
since poets are supposed to be
miserable, self-pitying wrecks
but nearly every morning
I wake up feeling really good.
I'm forty years old
and the only time I have ever had
'a proper job'
was for eleven months
sixteen years ago.
I'm a poet
I can earn a living as a poet
and I get to travel all over the world.
I love writing
I love the world
and I love to travel
so there isn't much of a problem.
Sometimes I'm away for weeks on end
and although most of the time
I hardly miss England at all
there is a part of me
which always looks forward to coming home.
Most of all, I miss my partner – her intelligence
sovereignty and inspiration
I miss a decent pint of real ale
I miss my beloved Brighton and Hove Albion
despite the fact we're crap
I miss my pet bullfrogs
and my pond
full of strangely voracious piscine delinquents

and although this may seem incongruous
for someone constantly portrayed
as an angry punk rock poet
I really miss my garden.
You see, I love gardening.
I'm a new wave gardener.
I love planting things and watching them grow.
I love the feeling of being close to the sea
and close to the soil.
And there's another side to all this.
There are things which turn me into a total horticultural psychopath
a ruthless agricultural megalomaniac
and not just me – all red-blooded gardeners
feel the same.
I'll tell you what they are:
WEEDS.
Now some woolly-minded liberal do-gooders
will tell you
that weeds
are just
'flowers growing in the wrong place.'
But I know better.
Weeds are scum.
Weeds are filthy, evil parasites.
Weeds are genetically impure renegades
freeloading on my carefully distributed
ecologically sound fertiliser
they have no right to exist
and they must DIE.

Or at the very least
Know Their Place.
Let them clog up railway sidings
and annoy the trainspotters
or eke out their miserable existences
on motorway central reservations
deprived of nutriments
and blasted by lead fumes.
These are their designated areas.
Now I'm not being excessive:
my resettlement plan
for these anarchistic subvegetables
is approved by the United Nations
and I have a peacekeeping compost heap
in place at all times
but whatever I try
whatever awesome penalties I introduce
however many black bin liners I fill
the weeds keep coming
and when I'm away
– on tour, abroad, whatever –
they regroup
organise a morale-boosting press conference
with the stinging nettles
in the overgrown alley
at the other side of the fence
and creep back.
Bindweed is the worst.
Bindweed really brings out the chetnik in me.

A final solution for bindweed
that's what I want.
I have a Zen Stalinist five year plan
for my little harbourside agricultural cooperative
and bindweed
chickweed
thistles
and crappy strands of stray grass
are not part of it.
And I'm sure any gardeners reading this
will agree with me.
I'm sure you don't like weeds
any more than I do.
I'm sure you've all turned your back gardens
into horticulturally pure areas – haven't you?
Ethnic cleansing.
Now there's a concept.

Southwick

Southwick is like Amsterdam
only smaller and quieter
there aren't any prostitutes or sex shops
New Model Army have never played here
very few people use illicit substances
and no-one commits adultery.
Southwick is like Amsterdam
except that when you walk through the Square
the people who ask you for money
have perms instead of dreadlocks
'crack' is something found in the pavements
that the nice Adur Council workmen missed
'heroine' is strictly an amateur dramatic role
and 'pavement' is a pavement
not a cultishly successful
American grunge band.
'Score' is something Southwick Football Club
do from time to time
'gay' means 'light-hearted or merry'
and 'dope' is someone
who has left their bus pass at home.
Terry and June have always lived in Southwick
Richard Briers thinks it's very nice
Monty Python visit occasionally
The Levellers' new CD was spotted
on sale in Woolworths once
and all the poets and socialists
were turned back at Hove.
Except me.
I guess I slipped through the net.

Southwick is like Amsterdam
except the power station only has one chimney
the second amputated, along with its body
in a very radical architectural mastectomy
and there's only one canal
but it does have rats though –
you can see them scurrying
around the jetties at dusk
which is lovely
and it's full of mullet in the summer
and quite a lot of flatfish too
which for a lover of flatfish like myself
if you mullet over
constitutes a ray of hope
since it's actually rather a brill and soleful
plaice
to write poetry
and there's a towpath
where you can skate too
if you're a dab hand at it
but be careful not to flounder over the edge
because the water is rather foul
and in October
there's often nearly as much scum on its surface
as there is at the Brighton Centre
just along the road
attending the Conservative Party Conference.
Southwick is like Amsterdam –
OK, Anne Frank didn't live here
and there aren't as many bicycles

and the Heineken's a lot weaker
and Ajax would be a little out of place
in the Sussex County League
but we've got a lot more flatfish.
And where there are flatfish
there's poetry.

Some of you may be familiar with MC Trainspotter,
the world's first ever rapping trainspotter.
Now I'd like to introduce his homeboy T-Dance,
Southwick's first gangsta rapper . . .

Don't Dis The 'Hood

I wrote this rap after someone talked crap about the
'Wick
– it made me sick
So I'm saying it loud and I want it to be
understood:
Yo! don't dis the 'hood . . .

You moved down to Brighton, you work in the media
You drink in the Arts Club, you go down Komedia
You think torture movies are really cutting edge
You don't eat chips, you eat potato wedge
You say that Damien Hirst shit's so cool
You wish you'd pickled sheep at art school
but you're the sheep on a non-stop fashion trip
Emperor's New Clothes? Oh, they're so hip
You live in North Laine, Dials or Kemptown
Or somewhere else you were told things are going down
And that's where you stay – you never ever rove
Well, once a year you may stray into East Hove
Like a sheep does when the shepherd's got pissed
You dissed us – well, now you get dissed
You think life stops west of the West Pier
Yo – we're the homies; you just moved here
You think you're cool and we're just so slack:
South Central Southwick MC bites back
One more time so you pick it up real good:
don't dis the 'hood . . .

27

Yo! I'm T-Dance, I'll be your tour guide
Four miles west big chimney harbourside
take the next right, under the rail bridge
that's where we chill – straight from the fridge
Southwick Square, and now you've hit town
Check the Barn, that's where it's going down
Poets North South East and West
Theatre, music, dance – we've got the best
Glastonwick's the summer place to be
Real music, real ale, real poetry
Lottery posse respect our cool stance
We don't rob banks – no, we get grants
six three seven thousand, that's the figure
fill a form, no need to squeeze a trigger
And there's real respect elsewhere in the 'hood
It's turning out good
No more crack wars – council filled them in
pavements are sound, ain't nobody trippin'
there's a gang truce that lasts for ever
homies drink cider by the shops together
check the hoes – they're in the hardware store
we dig the scene – we know what a hoe's for
Bollocks to your sad old Brighton basement
We're so hip you need a hip replacement!

One last time 'cos it needs to be understood:
Don't dis the 'hood!

Stornoway

Why did we come to Stornoway?
I do not know. I cannot say.
The sea is oil. The sky is grey.
It rains and rains and rains all day.
No pollack bite. No fiddles play.
Just techno in a sad cafe
a spotty waitress with a tray
and dull religion to obey.
I wish I was in Whitley Bay
up to my neck in Beaujolais
or prodding General Pinochet
with an extremely sharp épee
or modelling my knob in clay
while watching Galataseray
or somewhere different, anyway
because this place is quite manqué
and I do not intend to stay.
Oh dirty, ugly Stornoway . . .
devoid of bass and sole and ray
and cod, skate, plaice and mullet grey
I came to fish, hear music play –
It's crap! I'm going to go away!

Harrogate

At length expelled from Bradford Bus
for the first time in Harrogate
I vowed I would not make a Fuss
nor get Drunk, nor Expectorate

For Such Behaviour would not fit
this Rest Home for the Middle Classes
(I saw a quaint Optician's. It
dispensed 'Eye-Wear': yes, that means Glasses.)

Blue Rinse was everywhere, and Tea.
And under every Lady's Pillow
in this Hub of Complacency
The Fuhrer's Photo. Hail Portillo!

But then I found the Hostelry
in which the Poet was to read.
Oh Pain! Oh Sad Grotesquerie!
What Contrast was there here, indeed . . .

A Toilet in the midst of Taste.
A Foetid Cuckoo in the Nest.
The Landlord harassed, and in Haste.
The Beer just piss. I should have guessed.

He wasn't sure that I would come,
he said. Hence, no Publicity.
The Drinkers in this Awful Dive
wanted a Disco. They got me.

But, as you know, I do not shrink
from Challenges, and took them on.
I made most of the Punters think.
The rest played Pool, their braincells gone.

Then, in the middle of my Set,
some started up a Football Game.
I love Football in Poetry – yet
combined this way, it was a shame.

Still, they were Friendly Folk enough.
I took my Fee, as well I ought,
and even sold some tapes and stuff.
Then trundled off. My final thought

on Harrogate: Well, it looks nice.
Though living here must surely bore yer.
And, Poets All, take my Advice:
Stay well clear of the Honest Lawyer!

Slough in Summer

At Slough station
on the westbound platform waiting-room wall
a local 'tagger'
– graffiti artist –
has left his mark.
I'm sure that one of the few station staff
still employed by
the Pontius pilots of privatisation
must have interrupted him in mid-spray
because what should have been
a proud, if ephemeral, staking
of suburban Berkshire territory
reads like German to me.
'Wilkommen am Strande' it seems to say.
'Welcome to the beach.'

For the last three years (at least) Brighton & Hove Albion fans have been involved in a bitter and very high profile battle to save our football club. Our beloved Goldstone Ground is gone, destroyed, now a retail park; 'bought' by former chairman Archer for £56.25p, sold to one set of property developers for £7m, then re-sold by them for £24m a year later – and of course Brighton & Hove Albion didn't see a penny of the profit.

Our club has been ripped from the heart of our community, is languishing at the bottom of the league and, as I write this, playing 'home' games at Gillingham, in a different county, seventy miles away. We are currently battling to get planning permission for a new stadium.

Fifteen years ago we were in the top division and oh, so nearly won the FA Cup at Wembley. It's an unbelievable story, well documented in the national media – the worst example of the way our culture and the game we love is being turned into a mere cypher for predatory moneymen. And we point the finger of blame at one man.

The first of these two poems was distributed as an explanatory leaflet to residents in the Lancashire village of Mellor before and during a demonstration organised there by Brighton Independent Supporters' Association, which I co-founded in 1993. The second was written on the occasion of the last-ever game at the Goldstone Ground on April 26, 1997.

To the Good People of Mellor, Lancs.
Saturday October 5th 1996

We're here in your Village, as angry as hell
(If it happened to you, you'd be angry as well)
To call for the Prompt and Immediate Departure
From all of our lives of a certain Bill Archer
Who lives in your midst – Vinehouse Farm, Whinney Lane –
And causes unlimited Anguish and Pain . . .
So what has he done, perchance? Why are we here?
It's because of the Football Club we all hold dear.
He's the 'chairman' of Brighton. At wondrous expense
(All of Fifty-six Pounds – oh, and Twenty-five Pence)
In a Deal we can only describe as grotesque
(If it wasn't so wrong it would be Pythonesque)
This Archer got hold of the Shares in our Club
For the price of a happy weekend in the Pub
Then he sold off our Ground, so we'd nowhere to go
Tried to groundshare with Portsmouth – until we said NO!
Now we're right at rock bottom, with nowhere to play
But things will improve – if he'll just GO AWAY!

The Seagulls soared high once; we've thousands of Fans
A Consortium waiting, with loads of new Plans –
And one man from Mellor, of whom we want Rid
Is holding things up with his Fifty-six Quid.
All of Sussex can't stand him. The Councils. Police.
Even Tory MPs tell him 'Leave us in Peace!'
Our Local Newspaper's petition is clear:
'You're no Robin Hood, Archer – you're not wanted here!'
From Hastings to Chichester, one thing is plain:
If Archer's got Fans, so has Saddam Hussein!

If you like him in Mellor, well, that's up to you.
(I suppose it's conceivable three of you do)
But he's nothing to do with our Club or our Town
And he's outstayed his Welcome, and getting us down!
So we've come here, in peace, to your Village and Pub
To tell you what Archer has done to our Club
And now that you know what this Visit's about
Come, Mellor, and join us: WE WANT ARCHER OUT!

Goldstone Ghosts

As bulldozers close in upon our old, beloved home
and those who stand to profit rub their hands
so we gather here together in sad, angry disbelief
and for one last time our voices fill the stands.
This is no happy parting, but a battle-scarred farewell
though victory hopes are mingled with the tears
And I, like you, will stand here as the final whistle blows
with memories which echo down the years . . .

The Chelsea fans threw pennies. Old ones. Sharpened. I was eight.
A target in the South Stand with my dad
And he got rather battered as he held me close and tight
and confirmed my view that Chelsea fans were mad!
And there, on those old wooden seats, I learned to love the game
The sights and sounds exploded in my head
My dad was proud to have a son with football in his blood –
but two short years later, he was dead.

Eleven. I went on my own. (My friends liked chess and stuff.)
'Now don't go in the North Stand!' said my mum.
But soon I did. Kit Napier's corner curled into the net.
Oh god. The Bournemouth Boot Boys! Better run . . .
Then Villa in the big crunch game. A thirty thousand crowd.
Bald Lochhead scored, but we still won the day.
Then up, and straight back down again. Brian Powney,
brave and squat.
T.Rex, DM's and scarf on wrist, OK?

And then the world was wonderful. Punk rock and Peter Ward!
And sidekick 'Spider' Mellor, tall and lean.
The legendary Walsall game. Promotion. Riding high.
Southampton–Spurs: that stitch-up was obscene.
The final glorious victory. Division One at last!
Arsenal, first game, midst fevered expectation.
Those Highbury gods tore us to shreds; we learned the lesson well.
Steve Foster was our soul and inspiration!

Man City came, and Gerry Ryan waltzed through them to score
And mighty Man United bit the dust.
Notts Forest, and that Williams screamer nearly broke the net.
The Norwich quarter-final; win or bust!
And after Wembley, Liverpool were toppled one last time
The final curtain on those happy days.
And then the years of gradual, inexorable decline –
sadly, for some, the parting of the ways.

But we stayed true, as glory days turned into donkeys' years.
Young, Trusson, Tiltman, Farrington. Ee-aw!
A Wilkins free-kick briefly brought us hope. 'Twas not to be.
The rot was deep and spreading to the core.

We found our voice and Lloyd was gone. Hooray! But worse to come.
Though just how awful we were yet to know.
Dissent turned to rebellion and then to open war
as on the terrace weeds began to grow.

The Goldstone sold behind our backs! Enraged, we rose as one
against a stony Northern businessman.
We drew a line, and said: ENOUGH! And as the nation watched
the final battle for our club began.
We fought him to a standstill. Fans United. All for one.
A nation's colours joined: a glorious sight.
And, finally, the stubborn, stony Archer moved his ground
and made way for our own collective Knight.

The battle's only just begun, but we have won the war.
Our club, though torn asunder, will survive.
And I salute each one of you who stood up and said NO!
And fought to keep the Albion alive.
And one day, when our new home's built, and we are storming back
A bunch of happy fans without a care
We'll look back on our darkest hour and raise our glasses high
and say with satisfaction: WE WERE THERE.

But first we have to face today. The hardest day of all.
Don't worry if you can't hold back the tears!
We must look to the future, in dignity and peace
as well as mourn our home of ninety years.
For me the Goldstone has an extra special memory
of the football soulmate I so briefly had.
He christened me John Charles and taught me to love the game.
This one's for Bill. A poet. And my dad.

Veronica

Veronica was one of the best
a strong, independent, resourceful woman
perceptive, sensual and humanist, with a bullshit detector
so finely developed
you knew you couldn't get away with anything.
She was a fulcrum for her children
a rock of support for her friends
and inspired love and respect in everyone she met.
We talked about everything
far into the night
and when her cancer returned
and she began fighting it with the same zest for life
determination and optimism
which embued everything she did
we talked about that too –
the really important things
the fundamentals of existence.
She went unbowed through the operations and tests
and even when in terrible pain
she had time for us, for our lives
our concerns, our feelings
dispensing opinions and advice
just as she had always done.
We always knew she was popular
but not until September
when we gathered at the crematorium
did we realise just how many people loved her.
The place was as packed
as the Square in Harlow
on the night Carter did their secret gig there.
It was like the North Stand
when Brighton & Hove Albion
had a proper team

and a North Stand
and a ground.
Most people were trying to be cheerful
we always knew she wouldn't have wanted it
any other way
her kids were smiling bravely through their tears.
And then it began.

Oh, Veronica!
In your lust for life
it was clear that right until the very end
you didn't believe it would happen this soon.
Death was the last thing on your mind.
You wanted to live
and so thoughts of your funeral
how you would have wanted it to be
would never even have occurred to you.
I guess your kids, numb with grief
and your amiably unassuming ex-husband
wanted to make things as easy as possible
and just went along with some distant family tradition.
I never even knew you had a Catholic background.
On the few occasions we discussed religion
'the afterlife'
and associated topics
our views coincided completely, or so it seemed to me –
and this after the black hand had already
made its presence felt.
Maybe it wouldn't have bothered you
that the final celebration of your life
was turned into a travesty.
Perhaps, and totally in character, you'd have said
'I'll be dead, won't I? What will I care?'

But, in truth, I think it would have angered you
as it angered us.
Realising what was coming, my partner and I
shifted uneasily in our seats
as a florid Catholic priest took the stage.
Obviously used to much smaller gatherings
he saw this as the big one
he'd psyched himself up
a chance to save a few heathen souls
or maybe just a chance to show off.
Anyway, he started talking.
For a long time.
Not about Veronica, of course – he'd never met her
hers was just another coffin in a conveyor belt
another date in a diary
although he did of course say
that he'd met her family
a few days before
and that after a couple of hours
he felt he'd 'known them all his life . . .'
No, he talked about himself, his church
what he did all day
then he tried to talk about Veronica
and got her name wrong, calling her Pat.
Then he posthumously remarried her
to the aforementioned ex-spouse.
Then he talked about 'her faith'
(the supposed faith of a humanist he'd never met)
and how 'sustaining' it must have been
which made me angry, and queasy
and I steeled myself for the next bit.

Oh, yes, I knew the next platitude which was coming.
People had said the same thing to me
as a ten-year old, when my father died
but that didn't stem the surge of bile to my throat.
'Of course', he said, 'Veronica is now much happier
than we are –
she's gone to a better place.'
My nails dug into my palms.
I wanted to stand up and scream
'You charlatan! You fraud! You hypocrite!
This warm, lovely woman – mother, friend, lover –
is dead.
Cold.
Oblivious.
Gone forever.
In a few minutes her remains will be burnt.
We'll never see her again. She no longer exists.
I'll tell you how dead she is –
if there was one spot of life in her
she'd sit bolt upright in her coffin
and tell you to stop talking such a steaming pile
of false, patronising crap!
She's dead!
And she's in a better place than us?
We who are alive?
Breathing, thinking, hopefully loving, conscious . . .
however sad or lonely or underachieving or
inadequate
or happy, fulfilled, inspired, creative
aware – blood coursing, hearts beating
above all, aware!

You don't really believe all that nonsense yourself
do you, priest?
Because if you did, you'd have thrown yourself
under a bus long ago
so that you could go to that 'better place' too . . .
You're just a sick confidence trickster!
If someone pointed a gun at your head
and cocked the trigger
you'd beg for your life, just like any of us would
you wouldn't say 'Go on, make my day, send me to
that better place . . .'
you'd piss yourself and beg to live –
you don't believe a word you're saying!'
But of course, I said nothing
None of us said anything
No-one ever says anything like that
on such an occasion.
We just fidgeted, and remembered Veronica
in our own way
as the florid, winy-nosed, holy water-splashing fool
pontificated on
and I vowed once more
as I urge you all
to squeeze every last drop of sweetness
from this thing we have called Life.
To take it in all its richness and celebrate it.
To do everything we can to improve its quality for
all of us who share this planet – now.
To celebrate Life
because Life is what we are –
it's our one chance

all biological, empirical and, yes,
philosophical logic
tells us:
This is all there is –
make it worthwhile.

Later, after the funeral,
in Veronica's sitting room
where six weeks before I'd given
a copy of my book
to our friend, shrunken and grey
with the terrible mark of liver cancer
and wondered what the hell to write inside
– I put 'love and total solidarity'
and left it at that –
I talked to her ex–husband.
I'd never met him before.
In the way of many strong and passionate women
she'd divorced him gently some years previously
but they had remained friends
he obviously still cared deeply for her
and was terribly sad.
'Tomorrow', he said, 'we'll go to the little plot I've bought
and put the ashes in it
and then that's it.'
And the simple words of that gentle man
in their terrible, loving finality
contrasted so totally with the rubbish
which had gone before.
I looked at him
smiled slightly
said nothing.

Of course, in all the ways which make us human
in the best sense
that isn't it.
Memories of Veronica will live long
in the hearts of those who love her
her sterling genes will be passed on
through her children
in the way of our biology, our identity, our species
but yes, dear friend, of course . . .
The door clanged shut
We drove away from her home for the last time
Joy looked back once and quietly said
'Goodbye, Veronica.'
That was all.

Now that the Brave New Labour Dawn has arrived, let's hope that this verse documenting eighteen years of hell will soon be a historical document. Sadly, I'm not so sure . . .

Victoria Road (Winter 1995)

There was a time, before the Car
(a better time, some say, by far)
when Queen Victoria's Scept'red Arm
kept all her subjects safe from harm
(as long as they were Rich, of course)
and folk were flogged without remorse
for being Ill and being Poor
and eating Gruel and wanting More
and stealing Sheep and bits of Food
and, worst of all, for being Rude . . .
A Nicer Folk there'd never been –
their Lavatories were always clean
their well-scrubbed Kitchens bright and neat
and Table Legs veiled and discreet.
A people Thrifty, Kind, Select
And, most importantly, Correct . . .
I'm sure, Dear Reader, you will know
That this was Many Years ago
and such a State pure and sublime
bears no resemblance to our Time
Where Impoliteness (sad to say)
and Indiscretion rule the day
along with Sex and Canine Turds
and very many kinds of Words
which to the folk of Former Times
would have been Foul and Grievous Crimes!

Now in the Godless, Stinking Pit
in which we Hapless Folk all sit
Enveloped in the Hellish Flames
of Techno Beats and Video Games
There are some folk whose stated Ways
Hark right back to those far-off days.
'Tis not the Etiquette they seek
to ape, neither the understated Chic
but for Victoria Road they hanker
Unfettered rule of Boss and Banker
Cold Market Forces, shorn of care –
The Iron Fist of Laisser Faire.
They start their Plan in Earliest School
Where Endless Testing is the rule
Subservience a Hallowed Grail
and Creativity past the Pale.
Their aim in this is very clear.
By means of Ignorance and Fear
they seek to turn the Mass of Souls
into a race of Hapless Proles
Incapable of Sovereign Thought
Obsessed with Adverts, what they've Bought
and lost without a VDU –
the Drones in Milton Friedman's Zoo.
Hence their Curriculum so bland
which no Decent Teacher can stand
Hence Admonitions long and stern
that what you Are is what you Earn
Hence, too, distrust of Roaming Minds

Creative Thinkers of all kinds
called 'Chattering Classes' and thus scorned.
Oh, Albion, you have been warned!
Victoria Road is looming fast:
The die is very nearly cast
Unthinkables are coming true
Yes, every day, a new one-two
received, not with a howl of Rage
but Acquiescence, on the page
and on the street. Our Trusted Friends
now look to very different ends.
The Guardian? A sychophant
of power; emasculated, headless ant.
The BBC moans on its knees
undone by Tory appointees
and now a National Anaesthetic –
its dissident protests pathetic.
The TUC? A satellite dish.
A Vacant Stare, a long-dead Fish.
A nation's Rebels? On a hike
to Game Shows, Adverts and the like.
A Foul Corruption stalks the land
and Opposition is so bland
that Boyzone's well-groomed Pubic Hair
is Communistic by compare . . .
And worse to come. Portillo cites
the Poor, the Sick, now 'parasites'
and soon – the Workhouse? Spiv-scum power.
Banana Britain's darkest hour.

A slavering, slobbering pig-dog Press
Laps up, laughs off each new excess
A token slap, then back for more –
a Nation rotten to the Core.
I'll rage until my rage takes fire
'Gainst each Corrupt and Bloated Liar
I will not cease from Mental Fight
I spit upon their heartless Right
I vomit on the Twisted Code
which takes us down Victoria Road.

The Zen Stalinist Manifesto

Playing golf or being otherwise dull
with malice aforethought
watching TV for more than ten hours a week
discussing soap operas
(or any TV programmes or adverts
in the case of a stand-up comedian on stage)
and becoming obsessed with the work of
Quentin Tarantino
Damien Hirst
or William Burroughs
will become a criminal offence
punishable by five years' enforced participation
in a non-stop mime
juggling
and face painting workshop
in Slough.

The Berlin Wall will be rebuilt –
only five metres higher.
It will keep people out.
People like the World Bank
the International Monetary Fund
the Spice Girls
Price Waterhouse
Goldman Sachs
Jeffrey Archer
William Archer
Peter Mandelson
Helmut Kohl
and Boris Yeltsin.

Peter Lilley and Michael Portillo
will suffer immediate retrospective abortion.

In order to combat the increasing danger
to civilised society
posed by pig-ignorant
misogynistic
right-wing
testosterone-poisoned
road rage specialists
theme gulags will be introduced
for anyone who drives a van with scratches down the side
and shouts at or otherwise intimidates
lone women drivers at roundabouts
or buys shares in industries
which belonged to him in the first place.

These gulags will all be situated on Rockall
and will have three themes:
Saturday night in August on the Costa Del Sol
auction day at the used car emporium on Shoreham seafront
and happy hour in a Harlow theme pub.
All themes will run 24 hours a day
365 days a year
and inmates will be able to nominate their chosen
theme on arrival.
No theme changing will be allowed
but Clash albums
chess sets
and copies of 'The Ragged-Trousered Philanthropists'
will be available for rehabilitation purposes.

Tight security will be enforced.
Theme gulags will be surrounded by large, deep moats
filled with soya milk and real ale
guarded by pitbullfrogs
and kept under constant surveillance

by hundreds of high court judges
watching from carefully constructed ivory towers.

Boris Yeltsin will finally be recognised
as the traitor and Judas he is
and made to spend the rest of his days
cleaning out the toilets
at the Glastonbury Festival.
With his tongue.

Every Western government leader
and the entire staff of the United Nations
will be forced to walk naked
through the burnt-out towns
and mass graves
in what used to be the Socialist Federation of Yugoslavia
and then have the words
'Marshall Tito was right'
tattooed on their foreheads.

A Zen Stalinist National Curriculum
will be introduced into schools.
Albanian
– both dialects, Gheg and Tosk –
will become compulsory as a foreign language.
Reading Geoffrey Archer
and supporting Crystal Palace
will become not just highly illegal
but indicative of a disturbed mental state
requiring instant frontal lobotomy.

The Alarm will reform.
All school students will have to attend morning assembly
and sing the new National Anthem:
'68 Guns' by The Alarm.

Mike Peters of The Alarm
will become the new Welsh football manager
with David Icke as his assistant.

The Royal Family
will be allowed to remain as figureheads
but will have to join The Alarm.
Billy Bragg will become next in line to the throne
and rhythm guitarist in The Alarm.
All game show hosts
and everyone who works for the Sun
and the Times Literary Supplement
will be shot.
Their executions will be videoed
an acid house soundtrack will be added
and huge week-long parties
known as 'graves'
will begin.

Ken Livingstone and his pet newt Dennis
will become Prime Minister
and Chancellor of the Exchequer.
All privatised industries will be renationalised
without compensation
and a huge TV and poster campaign will be launched
saying simply
'Tell Sid tough shit.'
The Queen will be privatised
and promoted to lead singer of The Alarm.
The first Zen Stalinist Five Year Plan
will be published
declaring world peace and social surrealism
and the dark nightmare of monetarist madness
will finally come to an end.
For ever.

Welcome to Cyberia

This is the soundbite blipvert hyperscene
Digital bar code swipe card internet
(anally unretentive cyberpet
shits virtually on bleeping microscreen).
The wandering poet plies his ancient craft
via home page, mailing list and database
and poems on the Web in cyberspace . . .
The library's becoming over-staffed.

Not techno-nerd nor Luddite, I'll have fun.
I'll go on-line a while, then down the pub.
I'll never join the bedroom surfers' club
nor curse the global age that's now begun
And for the kid whose concentration span
is less than that of the great crested newt
(a fault in some who take the cyber-route)
this interactive poet has a plan.

A concentration campsite on the Net.
Sent there, you must log off and read a book.
'Yes, that strange thing with pages – take a look!
Cyberia welcomes you – no need to fret . . .
You're here to learn to concentrate, no less –
to think and reason existentially.
Three weeks of Jean-Paul Sartre, then you're free*
So get stuck in to Being and Nothingness!'

You can't catch VD from a VDU
and some have virtual sex, I understand
(the whole thing's getting rather out of hand
though in this instance the reverse is true)
But me, I'll e-mail, surf, do my home page
Then make love with my woman till I flop
and hope the Seagulls can avoid the drop –
A global poet, bonded to our age.

Or perhaps not – he never quite worked that one out

53

668 – Neighbour of the Beast

He's an interesting fellow
yes, I must give him his due . . .
Goats out in the garden
Goblins in the loo
No Jehovah's Witnesses
Never sees a priest
Party wall is rather warm –
Neighbour of the beast.

The Goth at number 667
always gets my post
He lives across the road of course
(with two bats and a ghost)
The postman never gets it right
I tell him: Listen, mate:
It's Satanist suburbia –
I live at 668!

He's a devil in the kitchen
Watch those speculators fry!
There's severed cocktail sausages
and homemade nipple pie
Tagliatelle made from tapeworms
from dogs recently deceased
And the barbecue never goes out:
Neighbour of the beast.

He's got a little waiting list
of folk he wants to see
for a special dinner party
lasting all eternity . . .
On the menu: Ian Paisley,
Selwyn Gummer and the Pope.
For dessert: baked ayatollah.
Enter here – abandon hope!

When Tories cross the floor to join Labour, there must be something wrong . . . And so far (March 1998) it's New Labour, New Tory!

The Blandford Forum

Our voice is still, our memories subside
A dream of quiet nothing spurs us on
Canute floats out to sea
then back in with the tide
Our hopes and expectations are long gone
Cries of Pyrrhic victory fade into a snore
as a freshly-laundered cockroach
crawls across the panelled floor

Hold the front page, light the lamp
there's a new face in the Labour camp
Talking of a slightly better day
Forged the thumbscrews, worked the racks
Cracked the whip across our backs
Now he's turned a pinker shade of grey

The boundaries set in stone
along the Walworth Road
Leave wit and anger voiceless at the door
The land is bland, the wan-eyed man is king
and so shall be for now and evermore
This is England, dear old England
beloved unto me
Land of dope and Tory
Single mother of the free

Hold the front page, light the lamp
There's a new face in the Labour camp
Flew to Oz to find a holy grail
Rupert rules, so sell your soul
Procol Harum protocol
Let's all turn a whiter shade of pale

Like plaice in the sand of Shoreham
they change to suit the tide
while the Laird of the Blandford Forum
takes history for a ride . . .
but it's what the customer wants

When Burnham Wood sprouts over Dunsinane
and Seagulls fly unhindered through the year
Canute will build a dam that's not made out of sand
while publicans serve hogsheads of free beer
When we stoke a Wapping fire to blacken out the Sun
Every Midas in the midden will be on the chicken run

Hold the front page, light the lamp
There's a new face in the labour camp
Actually, it seems, there's quite a few
Some might say it's a bit unfair
I say we should leave them there
till they turn a redder shade of blue . . .

(reprise)
Hold the front page, light the lamp
there's a new face in the labour camp . . .

Sarajevo

You don't have to sit back and watch psychopaths fight
The hand of friendship is usually right
Most people want peace and a home somewhere
they don't care about the thugs and their murderous stare
Now we knew this – and for forty years
a brand new way replaced traditional fears
Most people lived happily side by side
No place for terror, no need to hide
But it wasn't to the liking of the World Bank suits
who cheered when the tribes rediscovered their roots
They can handle torture, rape and death
if it opens up markets for the IMF . . .
and they're free now, oh they're free now
'a chance for individuals to compete'
Free now, oh they're free now –
fascists gun down children in the street

I remember the message from Amnesty:
it said the whole damn lot of them should be 'free'
no matter what they say, no matter what they do
'cos they're 'all entitled to their point of view'
The liberals cheered when the deed was done
now they cry in the face of the tank and the gun
and the arms manufacturers are having fun as well
growing fat on the profits of sectarian hell
Now we always saw it another way
for a hundred years, educate each day
and suppress the thugs and their murderous lie
keep the lid on the pot till the hate boils dry
But they're free now, oh they're free now:
the rape camp guards can have a Big Mac for tea
Free now, oh they're free now –
welcome to Western liberal democracy

There's 'freedom' in Bischofferode, in East Germany
– a town closed due to 'economic unviability'
The word has become meaningless, a travesty
for there can be no freedom without power for the free
. . . and that means more than shopping, actually

In Afghanistan in 1979
everybody swallowed the American line
Misogynists from the twelfth century
were 'freedom fighters' on TV
The Western world took them to their hearts
The Afghan nation was torn apart
and now everything's gone no-one seems to care
about the awful nightmare that's happening there
Women cower under veil and lash
Taliban rake in corporate cash
but the nine o'clock news has got nothing to say
The Commies have gone . . . everything's OK . . .
They're free now, oh they're free now
They freeze in Moscow, starve in Albania
Free now! Oh, they're free now!
Fascism, war, poverty, mafia . . .
Free now! Oh, they're free now!
Look 'freedom' up in the latest dictionary
Free now! Oh, they're free now!
It says: 'an IMF loan and a monetarist economy'

In East Berlin the satirists sing
'Auf die Dauer hilft nur Mauer'
– we want our wall back, we want our wall back,
can we have our wall back please?

Doggy on a String *(you know the tune)*

I'm going down the Academy, the Levellers are playing
'Scuse me, have you got 10p, mate, you won't catch me paying
With my doggy on a string
With my doggy on a string

I follow Chumbawamba and Tofu Love Frogs and
sometimes go to Blyth Power
If it's more than a quid at the door I sit outside
and glower
Meat eaters I just can't stand
though I've got a leather wristband . . .

I'm hitching up to Cambridge, the Strawberry Fayre
If it's free and they play badly I'll gladly be there
With my doggy on a string
With my doggy on a string

Most of the time I live in a squat – though
sometimes I stay with my mum
I smoke dope a hell of a lot – I've got chugnuts all round me bum
Joolz designed my tattoo
Cider is better than glue . . .

I'm going down the beanfield to get my revenge
on the pigs who kicked my head in last year at Stonehenge
With my doggy on a string
With my doggy on a string

I followed New Model Army round Europe on 38p a day
I travelled round in a motorised skip so I always
had somewhere to stay

I spent the summer up a tree
'Scuse have you got 10p . . .?

I'm going down the Academy, the Levellers are playing
'Scuse me have you got 10p, mate, you won't catch me paying
With my doggy on a string
With my doggy on a string . . .

Joseph Porter's Sleepinge Bagge

(Well, it is Very Olde)

I thought, perhaps, it was a Slug
maybe a Decomposing Rug
or some Huge Condom, clogged with Clagge –
it's Joseph Porter's Sleepinge Bagge . . .

A Mad Bacteriologist's Dream
Where Bell End Boursin reigns Supreme
and even Bedbugs Puke and Gagge –
it's Joseph Porter's Sleepinge Bagge . . .

The Outside festers and within
The Inside's Grey As Major's Skin
A Quilted Dustbin, or a Ragge –
It's Joseph Porter's Sleepinge Bagge . . .

No Launderette has crossed its Path
Folk Vomit in its Aftermath
There's Notebooks and a Railway Magge
In Joseph Porter's Sleepinge Bagge . . .

A Camel's Foreskin, by Compare
Smells Sweeter than the Alpine Air!
I'll tell you this: I'd never Shagge
In Joseph Porter's Sleepinge Bagge!

63

The Final Ablution

The first poem ever to be written in solidarity with a washing machine . . .

Stung by these Words so rudely bawled
to Protag's Old Machine it crawled
A scene too gruesome to be screened
The day the Sleepinge Bagge was cleaned . . .

Industrial agent was fetched
The traumatised Appliance retched
Inside, a Sewer slowly sloshed
The day the Sleepinge Bagge was washed . . .

A Tidal Wave of Helmet Brie
Flowed, festering, towards the Sea
And in it Plague Rats gaily preened
The day the Sleepinge Bagge was cleaned!

The Foetid Futon's Foreskin Feta
Caused many an Angry Greenpeace Letter:
'First Exxon Valdez – now this!'
The day the Hotpoint took the Piss . . .

And now the Horrid Thing is clean
and Lilac-Smelling and Pristine
There's still no way I'd ever Shagge
in Joseph Porter's Sleepinge Bagge!

The Nuptial Fireplace

(For Joseph and Annie)

The Tale I now impart to you
(improbable, perhaps, but true)
concerns a Dame who asked one day
to breathe the Quaggish Quilt's bouquet . . .

She did not flinch as Bagge came near
but sniffed without a hint of Fear –
Somehow, the Suppurating Sac
became an Aphrodisiac!

Unfathomable Chemistry
A Miracle of Alchemy!
Repository of Sweaty Scrotum
now turned into a Lovers' Totem . . .

Bestow upon the Happy Pair
a Garland of Gonad Gruyere!
For now they sleep, all safe and snug
beneath this rank Rim Roquefort Rug

united! Hail the glorious Bagge!
Beatify its Sacred Clagge!
And hang it, stuffed in Oaken Case
above the Nuptial Fireplace . . .

Shirley Porter's Sleeping Bag

Homes for Votes and Seats for Cash –
now she really cuts a Dash
down on Wandsworth's Old Main Drag . . .
It's Shirley Porter's Sleeping Bag!

Happiness and Joy abounds:
Fined Seventeen Million Pounds!
New home for a Tory Hag
is Shirley Porter's Sleeping Bag . . .

Bankrupt, homeless, at a Loss
And nobody gives a Toss!
There's Meths and a Big Issue Mag
in Shirley Porter's Sleeping Bag . . .

Victims cheer and say 'Relax –
you'll still pay no Council Tax!'
Pubic Lice are playing Tag
in Shirley Porter's Sleeping Bag . . .

Local Cats all gather round her
drawn by whiff of Ancient Flounder
We're all singing the Red Flag
round Shirley Porter's Sleeping Bag!

The Marxist Tomato Grower

He sits and waits
for his world to turn red.
He knows it will,
eventually,
but it's taking
a hell of a long time.

This Means Waugh

Auberon Waugh
is a terrible baugh.
But I'd still much rather
him than his father.

'Let me die a youngman's death' (Roger McGough)

Rogered! *(an affectionate poke)*

Oh Roger, Roger, OBE
for services to poetry!
Touched by the Empire's latest breath
You'll never die a youngman's death . . .
A twilight in a health resort
A nursing home, and a fine port.
And, at the end, an epitaph
in Dailies Mail and Telegraph!

Lines on the Solving of a Much-Discussed Sanitary Problem at a Major Rock Festival by moving it to a well-known US Sports Arena

Flushing Meadow, wild and free!
What a place for Glastonbury!
Hail the great hygienic plain!
Do the gig – then pull the chain . . .

Also available by Attila the Stockbroker

Books:

Scornflakes *(Bloodaxe, 1992)*
(I hope very much to organise a reprint of my 1985 Unwin collection,
'Cautionary Tales for Dead Commuters,' in the near future.)

CDs/cassettes:

The Siege of Shoreham *(Roundhead Records, 1996)* with Barnstormer

Attila's Greatest Hits *(1993)*

This Is Free Europe *(Terz Records, Germany, 1993)*

668 – Neighbour of the Beast *(Larrikin Records, Australia, 1993)*

Cheryl – A Rock Opera *(with John Otway – Strike Back Records, 1991)*

Live at the Rivoli *(Festival Records, Canada, 1990)*

There have been many others but they are now all deleted and the best of
everything is on the Greatest Hits release.

For information on any of these or to join my free mailing list which will
keep you informed about gig dates, forthcoming releases, etc – write to
ATTILA, PO BOX 668, PORTSLADE, E SUSSEX BN42 4BG.